Better Homes and Gardens®

ALL-TIME FAVORITE

Fish & Seafood recipes

On the cover: Favorite fish and seafood main dishes, front to back: *Mushroom Filled Fish Rolls* topped with *Bechamel Sauce* and *Occidental Stir-Fry* made with shrimp and nectarines. (See index for recipe pages.)

BETTER HOMES AND GARDENS® BOOKS

Editor: Gerald M. Knox
Art Director: Ernest Shelton

Food and Nutrition Editor: Doris Eby
Senior Food Editor: Sharyl Heiken
Senior Associate Food Editors:
    Sandra Granseth, Elizabeth Woolever
Associate Food Editors: Bonnie Lasater, Marcia
    Stanley, Joy Taylor, Pat Teberg, Diana Tryon
Recipe Development Editor: Marion Viall
Test Kitchen Director: Sharon Golbert
Test Kitchen Home Economists: Jean Brekke,
    Kay Cargill, Marilyn Cornelius,
    Maryellyn Krantz, Marge Steenson

Associate Art Directors: Randall Yontz,
    Neoma Alt West

Copy and Production Editors: David Kirchner,
    Lamont Olson, David Walsh
Assistant Art Director: Harijs Priekulis
Senior Graphic Designer: Faith Berven
Graphic Designers: Linda Ford,
    Sheryl Veenschoten, Tom Wegner

Editor in Chief: James A. Autry
Editorial Director: Neil Kuehnl
Group Administrative Editor: Duane Gregg
Executive Art Director: William J. Yates

All-Time Favorite Fish and Seafood Recipes

Editor: Marcia Stanley
Copy and Production Editor: Lamont Olson
Graphic Designer: Neoma Alt West

CONTENTS

1
2
3
4
5

FISH & SEAFOOD TIPS

Even if you're a novice at cooking fish and seafood you'll find everything you need to know in *Better Homes and Gardens All-Time Favorite Fish and Seafood Recipes.* The introduction features dozens of suggestions to help you be a wise buyer of fish and seafood. The recipes, coupled with special tips on preparation scattered throughout the book, are carefully written to guide you to savory results every time.

This book offers versatility. It gives you choices if you are watching the budget, if you are choosey about certain foods, or even if you live where it's difficult to get fresh fish and seafood. You'll find possibilities for canned, frozen, and fresh fish, and whenever possible, the recipes let you pick the one you prefer. And many recipes let you choose one of several fish or seafoods so you can cater to special tastes. Finally, there's a range of recipes to match any occasion, from an old standby like Tuna Noodle Casserole to a more elegant favorite like Lobster Quiche.

Buying and Storing Fresh Fish

Shopping for fish requires special care and knowledge, but it's not difficult if you recognize the characteristics of good quality fish.

When buying fresh whole fish, look at the skin, flesh, eyes, and gills. Shiny, taut skin and bright colors indicate freshness. As a fish begins to deteriorate the colors start to fade. When you lightly press the flesh of a fresh fish with your finger, it springs back and feels firm and elastic. Another indication of freshness is clear, bright, bulging eyes. If the gills have not been removed, check to see that they are red and free of slime. As a fish loses quality the red gills fade to pink, then gray, and finally to brown or dark green. Avoid buying fish with a strong or "fishy" odor. A fresh fish smells sweet.

When buying a fresh fish that has been dressed or cut into steaks, fillets, or chunks, ask these questions: Do the cuts have a fresh appearance with no drying out around the edges? And, as with whole fish, ask yourself: Does the fish smell sweet but not "fishy"? Is the flesh of the fish firm and elastic? Does it spring back when you lightly press on it? Ideally fresh fish should be cooked and served right away so that you can enjoy the flavor at its best. If necessary, however, the fish can be refrigerated for a couple of days.

Storing fish in finely crushed ice is not necessary if it is refrigerated at 31° to 32° F. However, if possible, it is advisable to pack whole, drawn, or dressed fish in finely crushed ice before refrigerating. This helps hold the temperature down and keeps the surface moist and in good condition. Large chunks of ice should not be used because they bruise the flesh. Cuts such as steaks, fillets, or butterfly fillets should not be stored directly on ice because a nutrient loss occurs when the flesh comes in contact with the ice. To avoid nutrient loss, fish cuts can be wiped with a damp cloth, wrapped in wax paper, and then stored in finely crushed ice in the refrigerator.

If you plan to store fish in a refrigerator with other foods, the fish (or the fish and ice) should be placed in a tightly covered container.

Buying and Storing Frozen Fish

If a retailer is careless, frozen fish may thaw and freeze repeatedly, causing a loss of flavor and a risk of spoilage. Watch for these signs of thawing and refreezing when purchasing frozen fish: Packages that are misshapen, packages that have torn wrappers, and packages that have frost or blood visible inside or outside.

Frozen fish should be kept at 0° F. or colder. If the fish was purchased frozen it should not be allowed to start to thaw between purchase and storage. Freezing fish lengthens storage time. Species containing a large proportion of fat to lean, such as salmon, mackerel, or lake trout, should not be stored longer than two months. The leaner species, such as cod, haddock, ocean perch, pike or smelt, may be stored up to six months.

The best way to thaw frozen fish is in the refrigerator in the original wrapping. A one-pound package takes about 24 hours to thaw. For faster thawing place wrapped packages under cold running water. This reduces thawing time to one or two hours for a one-pound package. Use thawed fish within a day. *Do not thaw fish at room temperature or in warm water.*

Many types of white-fleshed fish can be used interchangeably in recipes. In those cases the recipe does not specify a particular fish, such as haddock, but simply calls for fish fillets, fish steaks, dressed fish, etc. Those fish that are interchangeable in many recipes include: Alaska pollock, Atlantic pollock, cod, croaker, flounder, Greenland turbot, grouper, haddock, hake, halibut, ocean catfish, ocean perch, sea bass, sea trout, sole, and whiting.

Fish and Seafood Terminology

Shopping for fish and seafood can be confusing unless you understand the terms used for various market forms. Here are a few definitions that may help next time you shop:
Whole or round fish: Whole fish just as they come from the water.
Drawn fish: Whole fish with the internal organs removed (eviscerated).
Dressed or pan-dressed fish: Fish that have been eviscerated and scaled. The head, tail, and fins usually have been removed. Pan-dressed refers to smaller fish.

Fillets: Pieces of fish cut lengthwise along either side of the backbone. When cut from one side of a fish it is a single fillet.

Steaks: Pieces of fish that are cross sections of a large dressed fish. Steaks are usually ½ to 1 inch thick.

Butterfly fillet: A piece of fish that is two single fillets held together by a small piece of skin and meat.

Breaded or battered fillets: Fillets with a crumb or batter coating. They are available raw or cooked.

Breaded or battered portions: Uniform serving portions cut from blocks of frozen fish that are usually bone-free. Portions are available raw or cooked, both with crumb or batter coating.

Fish sticks: Uniform sticks cut from blocks of frozen fish that are usually bone-free. Sticks are available raw or cooked, both with crumb or batter coating.

Green shrimp: Raw shrimp in shells with the head removed.

Lobster tail: Meat from the tail portion of a lobster, usually sold in the shell.

Peeled and deveined shrimp: Shrimp removed from the shell and with the black sand vein removed.

Shucked oysters, clams or mussels: Oysters, clams or mussels that have been removed from their shells.

Recommended Cooking Methods

	baked	fried	sautéed	deep-fat fried	poached	steamed	stewed	grilled	broiled
bluegill		•	•	•				•	•
carp	•								
catfish	•	•	•	•	•	•	•		
cod	•	•	•	•	•	•	•	•	•
croaker	•	•	•	•	•	•		•	•
flounder	•	•	•	•	•	•	•	•	•
grouper	•	•	•	•	•	•	•	•	•
haddock	•	•	•	•	•	•	•	•	•
hake	•	•	•	•	•	•	•	•	•
halibut	•	•	•	•	•	•	•	•	•
lake perch	•	•	•	•				•	•
pollock	•	•	•	•	•	•	•	•	•
salmon	•				•	•	•	•	•
smelt	•	•	•	•				•	•
snapper	•				•	•	•	•	•
sole	•	•	•	•	•	•	•	•	•
trout	•	•	•					•	•
turbot	•	•	•	•	•	•	•	•	•
whitefish	•	•	•					•	•
whiting	•	•	•	•	•	•	•	•	•

Cooking Frozen Fish

Frozen fish, fillets, and steaks may be cooked without thawing if additional cooking time is allowed. To bake slices from a one-pound block of frozen fish, let the block stand at room temperature for 20 to 30 minutes. Bias-slice the block into 1-inch, ½-inch, or ¼-inch slices and bake in 450° oven till fish flakes easily when tested with a fork. Allow 15 minutes for 1-inch slices, 8 minutes for ½-inch slices, and 5 minutes for ¼-inch slices.

Packages of individual fillets also may be cooked from the frozen state by placing the fillets in a shallow baking pan and baking them, uncovered, in a 450° oven until the fish flakes easily when tested with a fork. Allow 15 minutes for ½-inch-thick fillets and 10 minutes for ¼-inch-thick fillets.

To poach fish that is still frozen, allow the block to stand at room temperature for 20 to 30 minutes. Bias-slice the block into 1-inch, ½-inch, or ¼-inch-thick slices or into 1-inch cubes. Place the frozen fish in a greased skillet and add enough liquid to cover. Bring to boiling; reduce heat. Cover and simmer till fish flakes easily when tested with a fork. Allow 5 minutes for 1-inch slices, 2 minutes for ½-inch slices, 1½ minutes for ¼-inch slices, and 4 minutes for 1-inch cubes. Individually frozen fillets may be poached using the same method, but allow 8 minutes for ½-inch-thick fillets and 4 minutes for those ¼ inch thick.

Fish and Seafood Sauces

Choose one of these sauces to serve with a basic fish or seafood recipe. You'll find it adds variety, brings out the flavor, and enhances the appearance.

Tartar Sauce: Combine 1 cup *mayonnaise*, ¼ cup finely chopped *sweet pickle*, 1 tablespoon finely chopped *onion*, 1 tablespoon snipped *parsley*, 1 tablespoon chopped *pimiento*, and 1 teaspoon *lemon juice*. Chill thoroughly to blend flavors. Makes about 1 cup sauce.

Tomato Sauce: In a small saucepan cook 2 tablespoons chopped *onion* and 2 tablespoons chopped *green pepper* in 1 tablespoon *butter* till tender. Stir in 1 teaspoon *cornstarch*, 1 teaspoon *sugar*, a dash *garlic salt*, and a dash *pepper*. Add one 7½-ounce can undrained *tomatoes*, cut up; 1 tablespoon sliced *pimiento-stuffed olives*, and 1 tablespoon prepared *horseradish*. Cook and stir till bubbly. Makes about 1 cup sauce.

Tropical Tartar Sauce: In small mixing bowl combine ½ cup dairy *sour cream*, 1 tablespoon *milk*, ¼ teaspoon *celery salt*, and ¼ teaspoon *dry mustard*. Add ½ of a small *lemon*, peeled, sectioned, and finely chopped; ¼ cup drained crushed *pineapple*, 2 tablespoons finely chopped *green pepper*, and 1 tablespoon finely chopped *onion*. Mix well. Cover and chill. Makes about 1 cup sauce.

Veloute Sauce: Melt 2 tablespoons *butter;* stir in 3 tablespoons all-purpose *flour*. Add 1 cup *chicken broth or fish stock* and ⅓ cup *light cream* all at once. Cook and stir till bubbly; cook and stir 2 minutes more. Makes about 1⅓ cups sauce.

Wine Mornay Sauce: In saucepan melt 3 tablespoons *butter;* stir in 3 tablespoons all-purpose *flour*, ½ teaspoon *salt*, ⅛ teaspoon ground *nutmeg*, and a dash *pepper*. Add 1¼ cups *light cream* all at once. Cook and stir till thickened and bubbly; cook and stir 2 minutes more. Stir in ¼ cup dry *white wine*. Add ⅓ cup shredded *Swiss cheese;* stir till melted. Makes about 1¾ cups sauce.

Buying and Storing Seafood

Buying seafood is easy if you know what to look for.

Shrimp: Fresh shrimp have a mild odor. The meat is firm and the shell may be grayish green, pinkish tan, or light pink depending on the type of shrimp. Do not buy fresh *raw* shrimp that are reddish or dark pink. Fresh shrimp may have small areas of black coloration on the shell, but don't buy shrimp that have large areas of this "black spot."

Frozen shrimp can be purchased in several forms. As with most frozen products check the package for signs of damage. Ice crystals indicate previous thawing and refreezing. White spots on the contents indicate freezer burn.

Shrimp are sold by size or the number per pound. Larger shrimp are more expensive. Varying sizes often work interchangeably in a recipe, so you can get more for your money by using smaller shrimp. But sometimes it is necessary to use a specific size, such as in stuffed shrimp. When a particular size is important, the recipe will call for it.

After purchasing fresh shrimp, wash them thoroughly in cold water; place them in a covered container in the refrigerator. Shrimp will last 4 days.

Oysters: If you are buying oysters in the shell, be sure they are alive by checking to see that the shell is tightly closed. If it is open, tap it. If the oyster is alive, the shell will quickly close. Do not buy oysters whose shells will not close.

Shucked oysters should be plump and have a clear liquid. The color of fresh oysters should be creamy or gray-brown. A high proportion of liquid is an indication of improper handling and results in bloating of the oysters, partial loss of flavor, and some loss of food value.

Oysters in the shell will last two to three weeks if kept on ice or in the refrigerator. Shucked oysters will keep seven to ten days if refrigerated.

Clams: Clams in the shell should be alive when purchased. If they are alive, the shell will be tightly closed or will close when you tap it. Clams that will not close or those with cracked or broken shells should be rejected.

Shucked clams are plump and not shriveled when fresh. The liquid should be clear and contain no shell pieces.

Crabs and Lobsters: If you buy live crabs or lobsters be sure they are alive and will move their legs when touched. The tail of a live lobster will curl under its body and not hang down when you pick it up.

Crabs and lobsters cooked in the shell should be bright red and have no disagreeable odor. By lifting the lid under the body section of crabs it is easy to detect any odor.

Scallops: When buying fresh scallops, check for a sweet odor. Frozen scallops also have a sweet odor after they are thawed. Large sea scallops have white meat, while smaller bay scallops can be creamy white, light tan, or pinkish. Scallops packaged in containers should have little if any liquid.

No matter what kind of fish or seafood you purchase, keep it refrigerated at all times.

1 FROM THE OVEN

Many types of fish and seafood easily lend themselves to oven cookery. On the following pages you'll find soufflés, casseroles, whole fish, fillets, appetizers, and more. Add to your fish and seafood recipes from our assortment of favorites.

Baked Fillets and Steaks

2 **pounds fresh or frozen fish fillets or steaks**
3 **tablespoons butter or margarine, melted**
Lemon wedges (optional)

Thaw fish, if frozen. Cut fillets into 6 serving-size portions. Place fish in greased baking pan in single layer with skin side down. Tuck under thin edges. Brush tops with melted butter or margarine. Season with salt and pepper. Bake, uncovered, in 450° oven until fish flakes easily when tested with a fork. (Allow 5 to 6 minutes for each ½ inch of thickness.) If desired, serve with lemon wedges. Makes 6 servings.

Oven-Fried Fish

3 **10- to 12-ounce fresh or frozen pan-dressed trout or other fish or 1 pound fresh or frozen fish fillets or steaks**
1 **beaten egg**
½ **cup fine dry bread crumbs**
¼ **cup butter, melted**
1 **tablespoon lemon juice**

Thaw fish, if frozen. If using fillet block, cut block into 3 or 4 pieces. Dip fish into beaten egg, then into bread crumbs. Place coated fish in a well-greased, shallow baking pan; season with salt and pepper. Combine melted butter and lemon juice; drizzle over fish. Bake in 500° oven until golden and fish flakes easily when tested with a fork. (Allow 5 to 6 minutes for each ½ inch of thickness.) Makes 3 or 4 servings.

Fillets in Wine

1 **pound fresh or frozen fish fillets**
1 **large tomato, peeled and thinly sliced**
¼ **cup dry white wine**
½ **teaspoon dried basil, crushed**
½ **cup shredded American, Swiss, or Gruyère cheese (2 ounces)**

Thaw fillets, if frozen. Place fillets in greased 11x7x1½-inch baking pan. Season with salt and pepper. Arrange tomatoes on top; sprinkle with additional salt. Carefully pour wine over all; sprinkle with basil. Bake in 350° oven for 20 minutes. Sprinkle with shredded cheese and bake 5 to 10 minutes longer or until fish flakes easily when tested with a fork. Transfer to serving platter, spooning some of the juices atop. Makes 4 servings.

Baked Fish St. Peter

2 **pounds fresh or frozen fish fillets**
Olive oil or cooking oil
Paprika
3 **cups sliced fresh mushrooms**
1 **14-ounce can artichoke hearts, drained and halved**
Eggplant-Tomato Sauce
Hot cooked rice (optional)

Thaw fish, if frozen. Place fish in 13x9x2-inch baking dish. Brush with a little oil; sprinkle with paprika, salt, and pepper. Bake, uncovered, in 400° oven for 15 minutes. Add mushrooms and artichokes; spoon Eggplant-Tomato Sauce over all. Cover; return to oven and bake for 20 minutes. Uncover; bake about 5 minutes more. If desired, serve with hot cooked rice. Makes 8 servings.

Eggplant-Tomato Sauce: In saucepan combine one 16-ounce can *tomatoes,* cut up; 1 cup peeled and chopped *eggplant;* ¾ cup *vegetable juice cocktail;* ½ cup chopped *onion;* ¼ cup chopped *celery;* ¼ cup dry white *wine;* 1 small fresh *chili pepper,* seeded and chopped; 2 tablespoons snipped *parsley;* 2 tablespoons *olive oil or cooking oil;* 1 tablespoon *Worcestershire sauce;* 2 teaspoons *sugar;* 1 teaspoon dried *basil,* crushed; ¼ teaspoon dried *thyme,* crushed; and ¼ teaspoon dried *oregano,* crushed. Bring to boiling; reduce heat. Boil gently, uncovered, about 40 minutes or till slightly thickened. Stir sauce occasionally.

Fiesta Salmon (see recipe, page 19) features chili peppers and tortilla chips.

Spanish-Style Fish (pictured on page 26)

2 **pounds fresh *or* frozen fish steaks**
2 **medium tomatoes, sliced**
½ **small cucumber, sliced**
¼ **cup chopped onion**
¼ **cup chopped green pepper**
1 **clove garlic, minced**
2 **tablespoons butter**
2 **tablespoons snipped parsley**
2 **tablespoons lemon juice**
½ **teaspoon dried marjoram, crushed**

Thaw fish, if frozen. Place fish steaks in greased baking dish. Arrange tomato and cucumber slices atop. In saucepan cook onion, green pepper, and minced garlic in butter till onion is tender but not brown. Remove from heat; stir in parsley, lemon juice, and marjoram. Spoon over fish. Bake in 375° oven about 25 minutes or until fish flakes easily when tested with a fork. Makes 6 servings.

Catfish with Italian Sauce

3 **1-pound fresh *or* frozen dressed catfish *or* other fish**
1 **8-ounce can tomato sauce**
1 **tablespoon cooking oil**
½ **teaspoon sugar**
½ **teaspoon dried basil, crushed**
⅛ **teaspoon garlic powder**
¼ **cup grated Parmesan cheese**

Thaw fish, if frozen. Place in well-greased shallow baking dish. Cover with foil. Bake in 350° oven for 35 to 40 minutes or until fish flakes easily when tested with a fork. Meanwhile, in small saucepan combine tomato sauce, oil, sugar, basil, garlic powder, and ¼ teaspoon *salt*. Bring to boiling; reduce heat. Simmer, uncovered, about 5 minutes.

Drain excess liquid from baking dish. Spoon tomato sauce mixture over fish; sprinkle with Parmesan. Bake 5 minutes longer. Remove to serving platter. Makes 6 servings.

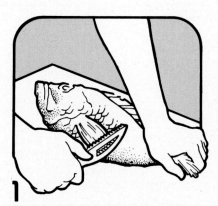

1
To clean a small fish, first remove the scales. Using a table or solid surface, hold the fish firmly with one hand. Do not allow the fish to slide as you work. With the other hand, use a knife or scraper and work from tail to head to scrape off the scales.

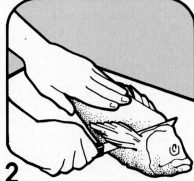

2
With a sharp knife cut from the top of the head down through the spine, cutting behind the gills on both sides of the fish. Pull the head down, removing the internal organs (entrails) with the head.

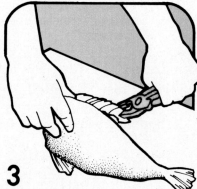

3
Using pliers, with a forward motion pull toward the head end to remove the top and bottom fins. Use a sharp knife to cut off the tail fin. Thoroughly wash the fish, being sure that all the blood and the scales are washed away.

Fish Topped with Clam Stuffing

2 pounds fresh *or* frozen fish
   fillets
¼ cup sliced green onion
¼ cup butter *or* margarine
1 8-ounce package (2 cups)
   herb-seasoned stuffing mix
1 6½-ounce can minced clams

Thaw fish, if frozen. Cook onion in butter till tender; remove from heat. Add stuffing mix and *undrained* clams. (If mixture is dry, add 1 to 2 tablespoons water.) In greased 13x9x2-inch baking dish arrange fillets in single layer. Spoon clam mixture on each; press lightly. Bake in 350° oven 20 to 25 minutes or until fish flakes easily when tested with a fork. Transfer to platter. Makes 6 servings.

Fish in Cheese Sauce

1 pound fresh *or* frozen fish
   fillets *or* steaks
1 tablespoon butter, melted
1 10-ounce package frozen cut
   asparagus
2 tablespoons butter
2 tablespoons all-purpose flour
¼ teaspoon salt
1 cup milk
½ cup shredded *process* Swiss
   cheese
½ cup shredded American cheese
1 cup soft bread crumbs
2 tablespoons butter, melted

Thaw fish, if frozen. If necessary, cut into serving-size pieces. Place fish in single layer in well-greased 10x6x2-inch baking dish. Tuck under thin edges. Brush with 1 tablespoon melted butter; season with salt and pepper. Bake in 450° oven until fish flakes easily when tested with a fork. (Allow 5 to 6 minutes for each ½ inch of thickness.)

Meanwhile, cook asparagus according to package directions; drain. Set aside. In saucepan melt 2 tablespoons butter; stir in flour, salt, and dash *pepper*. Add milk all at once; cook and stir till bubbly. Remove from heat; stir in cheeses. Place asparagus on top of fish; pour cheese mixture over all. Combine bread crumbs and 2 tablespoons melted butter; sprinkle atop. Continue baking 5 to 8 minutes or till lightly browned. Makes 4 servings.

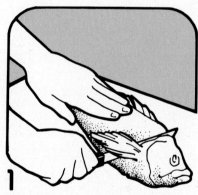

1 To fillet a fish, hold it firmly by its body. Insert a sharp knife into the fish diagonally behind the top of its head. Cut from the top of the head down to the spine, cutting behind the gills.

It is especially important to use a well-sharpened knife to fillet and skin fish.

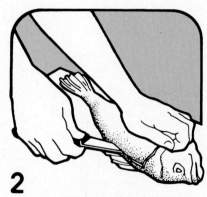

2 Be certain that the knife blade is placed on top of the spine and rib cage. Cut the meat as close to the spine and rib cage as possible by sliding the knife from the cut behind the head and gills toward the tail.

3 To skin the fillet start at the tail end and insert a sharp knife between the meat and skin. Firmly hold the skin and use a sawing motion with the knife to cut the meat away from the skin. Repeat all three steps on the other side of the fish.

Egg-Stuffed Fish Rolls

1 **pound fresh *or* frozen fish fillets**
3 **hard-cooked eggs, chopped**
2 **tablespoons snipped parsley**
2 **tablespoons mayonnaise**
1½ **teaspoons Dijon-style mustard**
1 **10-ounce package frozen chopped broccoli, thawed**
2 **cups cooked rice**
1 **10¾-ounce can condensed cream of shrimp soup**
½ **cup dry white wine**

Thaw fish, if frozen; separate fillets. Cut and piece together to make four 6x2½-inch strips. Season fish with salt and pepper. Combine hard-cooked eggs, parsley, mayonnaise, and mustard. Spoon *3 to 4 tablespoons* of the egg mixture atop each fillet; roll up.

Combine broccoli and cooked rice. In bowl stir together soup and wine. Stir *1 cup* of the soup mixture into rice mixture. Turn rice mixture into 10x6x2-inch baking dish. Place fish rolls atop rice. Pour remaining soup mixture over rolls. Cover with foil; bake in 375° oven for 25 minutes. Uncover; bake 10 to 15 minutes more or till fish flakes easily when tested with a fork. Makes 4 servings.

Fish and Swiss Bake

1 **pound fresh *or* frozen fish fillets**
2 **tablespoons snipped parsley**
½ **cup shredded Swiss cheese**
1 **tablespoon butter *or* margarine**
1 **tablespoon all-purpose flour**
¼ **teaspoon salt**
Dash pepper
½ **cup evaporated milk**
2 **tablespoons dry sherry**

Thaw fish, if frozen; separate fillets. Cut and piece together to make four 6x2½-inch strips. Sprinkle with parsley and a little salt; top each strip with *1 tablespoon* of the cheese. Roll up jelly-roll fashion. Place rolls in 8x8x2-inch baking dish. In saucepan melt butter; stir in flour, salt, and pepper. Add milk and sherry all at once; cook and stir till thickened and bubbly. Pour over fillets. Bake, uncovered, in 400° oven 30 to 35 minutes or till fish flakes easily when tested with a fork. Sprinkle with remaining cheese; return to oven for 2 to 3 minutes or till cheese melts. If desired, garnish with additional parsley. Makes 4 servings.

Stacked Fillets

2 **pounds fresh *or* frozen fish fillets**
2 **cups sliced fresh mushrooms**
3 **tablespoons sliced green onion**
1 **clove garlic, minced**
2 **tablespoons butter *or* margarine**
1 **6½-ounce can minced clams, drained**
2 **tablespoons snipped parsley**
1 **tablespoon lemon juice**
¾ **teaspoon dried oregano, crushed**
¼ **teaspoon salt**
⅛ **teaspoon pepper**
Shrimp Sauce *or* Bechamel Sauce
Parsley sprigs (optional)
Lemon wedges (optional)

Thaw fish, if frozen. Cook mushrooms, green onion, and garlic in butter or margarine till tender. Remove from heat; stir in drained clams, 2 tablespoons parsley, lemon juice, oregano, salt, and pepper. In 13x9x2-inch baking dish place half the fish fillets in a single layer. Spoon mushroom mixture over each fillet. Stack with remaining fillets. Bake, uncovered, in 350° oven for 25 minutes; uncover and bake 10 to 15 minutes more or till fish flakes easily when tested with a fork. With slotted spatula transfer fish stacks to oven-proof serving platter. Serve with Shrimp Sauce or Bechamel Sauce. Garnish with parsley sprigs and lemon wedges, if desired. Makes 6 to 8 servings.

Shrimp Sauce: Combine 2 tablespoons melted *butter or margarine*, 2 tablespoons snipped *parsley*, and 1 tablespoon *lemon juice*. Drain one 4½-ounce can tiny *shrimp*; stir into mixture. Spoon atop fish. Bake in 350° oven till hot.

Bechamel Sauce: Cook ¼ cup finely chopped *onion* in 1 tablespoon *butter or margarine* till tender. Stir in 1 tablespoon all-purpose *flour*, ½ teaspoon *salt*, and dash *white pepper*. Add 1¾ cups *milk* all at once; cook and stir till thickened and bubbly. Cook and stir 2 minutes more. Stir *half* the hot mixture into 3 slightly beaten *egg yolks*. Return all to pan. Cook and stir over low heat for 2 to 3 minutes. Spoon over fish.

Egg-Stuffed Fish Rolls, baked atop broccoli and rice, and *Stacked Fillets,* filled
with mushrooms, green onion, and minced clams, turn fish fillets into special entrées.

Florentine Fillets

1 **pound fresh *or* frozen fish fillets**
1 **10-ounce package frozen chopped spinach**
1 **4-ounce container whipped cream cheese with pimientos**
1 **tablespoon butter *or* margarine**
4 **teaspoons all-purpose flour**
1 **teaspoon instant chicken bouillon granules**
1 **tablespoon dry white wine Paprika**

Thaw fish, if frozen. Cook spinach according to package directions; drain well. Spread spinach in 9-inch pie plate. Separate fillets; cut and piece together to make four 6x2½-inch strips. Season with salt and pepper. Spread *half* the cream cheese atop fillets. Roll up each fillet and place on top of spinach.

In saucepan melt butter; stir in flour, bouillon granules, ⅛ teaspoon *salt,* and dash *pepper.* Add ¾ cup *water;* cook and stir till thickened and bubbly. Remove from heat and gradually stir into remaining cream cheese; stir in wine. Pour over fillets. Sprinkle with paprika. Bake in 350° oven for 20 to 25 minutes. Makes 4 servings.

Cheesy Fish Casseroles

1 **pound fresh *or* frozen fish fillets**
¼ **cup finely chopped onion**
2 **tablespoons butter**
2 **tablespoons all-purpose flour**
¼ **teaspoon salt**
⅛ **teaspoon pepper**
1½ **cups milk**
1 **cup shredded American cheese**
1 **1½-ounce envelope cream sauce mix**
1 **cup frozen peas, thawed**
1 **4-ounce can mushroom stems and pieces, drained**
2 **tablespoons butter**
1½ **cups soft bread crumbs**

Thaw fish, if frozen. In large skillet barely cover fillets with water. Simmer for 12 to 15 minutes or until fish flakes easily when tested with a fork; drain. Break fish into large chunks; set aside.

Meanwhile, in a large saucepan cook onion in 2 table-spoons butter till tender but not brown. Stir in flour, salt, and pepper. Add *1 cup* of the milk all at once. Cook and stir till thickened and bubbly. Remove from heat. Add cheese; stir till melted.

Using the ½ cup milk, prepare sauce mix according to package directions. Stir in cheese mixture, fish, peas, and mushrooms. Turn into six 8-ounce shallow casseroles. Melt remaining 2 tablespoons butter; toss with bread crumbs to combine. Sprinkle atop casseroles. Bake, uncovered, in 400° oven for 15 to 20 minutes. Garnish each with parsley and paprika, if desired. Makes 6 servings.

Stuffed Fish

2 **pounds fresh *or* frozen fish fillets**
1 **3-ounce can chopped mushrooms**
  Milk
¼ **cup chopped onion**
¼ **cup butter *or* margarine**
1 **7-ounce can crab meat, drained, flaked, and cartilage removed**
½ **cup coarsely crushed saltine crackers**
2 **tablespoons snipped parsley**
½ **teaspoon salt**
  Dash pepper
3 **tablespoons butter**
3 **tablespoons all-purpose flour**
⅓ **cup dry white wine**
1 **cup shredded Swiss cheese**
½ **teaspoon paprika**

Thaw fish, if frozen. Separate fillets; cut and piece together to make eight 6x2½-inch strips. Drain mushrooms, reserving liquid. Add enough milk to reserved mushroom liquid to make 1½ cups total liquid; set aside. In skillet cook onion in ¼ cup butter or margarine till tender but not brown. Add drained mushrooms, flaked crab meat, cracker crumbs, parsley, salt, and pepper; mix well. Spread mixture over fish strips. Fold fish strips over filling; tuck end under and place fish, seam side down, in 12x7½x2-inch baking dish.

In saucepan melt 3 tablespoons butter. Stir in flour and ¼ teaspoon *salt.* Add the reserved 1½ cups liquid and wine to saucepan. Cook and stir till thickened and bubbly. Pour over fillets. Bake in 400° oven about 30 minutes or until fish flakes easily when tested with a fork. Sprinkle with Swiss cheese and paprika. Return to oven. Bake about 5 minutes longer or till cheese is melted. Makes 8 servings.

Baked Stuffed Salmon

1½ cups sliced fresh mushrooms
1 cup shredded carrot
¼ cup sliced green onion
¼ cup snipped parsley
¼ cup butter *or* margarine
1 6-ounce package regular long grain and wild rice mix
2½ cups water
2 teaspoons instant chicken bouillon granules
⅛ teaspoon pepper
1 5-pound dressed salmon
3 tablespoons butter *or* margarine, melted

In saucepan cook mushrooms, carrot, onion, and parsley in ¼ cup butter or margarine till tender. Add rice and seasonings from mix; mix well. Stir in water, bouillon granules, and pepper. Cover; cook over low heat about 25 minutes or till rice is tender and liquid is absorbed.

Rinse fish and pat dry. Place in greased 15½x10½x2-inch baking pan. Brush 3 tablespoons melted butter or margarine on inside and outside of fish; sprinkle fish cavity with salt and pepper. Stuff loosely with rice mixture. (Spoon extra rice mixture into small casserole. Bake, covered, last 30 to 40 minutes of baking time.) Bake stuffed fish, covered, in 350° oven about 1½ hours or till fish flakes easily when tested with a fork. Makes 8 servings.

Luau Fish Bake

1 1- to 1½-pound fresh *or* frozen dressed fish
½ cup sliced celery
¼ cup chopped green pepper
2 tablespoons chopped onion
3 tablespoons butter *or* margarine
1½ cups herb-seasoned stuffing mix
3 tablespoons water
Lemon juice
1 tablespoon brown sugar
1 teaspoon cornstarch
2 tablespoons water
2 tablespoons lemon juice
2 tablespoons soy sauce
2 tablespoons sliced green onion
1 tablespoon butter *or* margarine
1 clove garlic, minced

Thaw fish, if frozen. Cook celery, green pepper, and chopped onion in 3 tablespoons butter or margarine till tender but not brown. For stuffing mixture combine vegetables, stuffing mix, and 3 tablespoons water.

Place fish on well-greased foil; season cavity with salt and brush with lemon juice. Stuff cavity with stuffing mixture. Seal foil around fish. Place in shallow baking pan. Bake in 350° oven for 30 minutes. Turn foil back; continue baking for 10 to 15 minutes or till fish flakes easily when tested with a fork.

Meanwhile, for sauce, in small saucepan combine brown sugar and cornstarch. Stir in 2 tablespoons water, 2 tablespoons lemon juice, and soy sauce. Add green onion, 1 tablespoon butter or margarine, and garlic. Cook and stir till thickened and bubbly. Remove fish to warm serving platter. Pour sauce over fish. Makes 3 servings.

Red Snapper with Wild Rice Stuffing (pictured on page 18)

1 3-pound fresh *or* frozen red snapper *or* other fish (with head and tail)
1 4-ounce package wild rice
1 cup sliced fresh mushrooms
¼ cup butter *or* margarine
1 cup frozen peas, thawed
2 tablespoons sliced green onion
2 tablespoons chopped pimiento
½ teaspoon finely shredded lemon peel
2 tablespoons lemon juice
2 tablespoons butter *or* margarine, melted

Thaw fish, if frozen. Cook rice according to package directions. Cook mushrooms in ¼ cup butter or margarine till tender. For stuffing combine cooked rice, cooked mushrooms, peas, green onion, pimiento, lemon peel, lemon juice, 1 teaspoon *salt,* and ⅛ teaspoon *pepper.* Toss lightly.

Sprinkle fish cavity with salt. Fill fish cavity with stuffing, patting stuffing to flatten evenly. Tie or skewer fish closed; place in a greased large shallow baking pan. Brush some of the 2 tablespoons melted butter over fish. Bake in 350° oven for 45 to 60 minutes or till fish flakes easily when tested with a fork, brushing occasionally with remaining melted butter. Carefully lift fish to warm platter. Remove string or skewers. Garnish with lemon slices and bias-sliced green onions, if desired. Makes 6 servings.

Crab-Stuffed Chicken

4 whole large chicken breasts,
      skinned, boned, and halved
      lengthwise
3 tablespoons butter *or*
      margarine
¼ cup all-purpose flour
1 teaspoon instant chicken
      bouillon granules
¾ cup water
¾ cup milk
⅓ cup dry white wine
¼ cup chopped onion
1 tablespoon butter *or* margarine
1 7-ounce can crab meat,
      drained, flaked, and cartilage
      removed
1 4-ounce can chopped
      mushrooms, drained
½ cup coarsely crushed saltine
      crackers
2 tablespoons snipped parsley
½ teaspoon salt
   Dash pepper
1 cup shredded Swiss cheese
½ teaspoon paprika

Place 1 chicken piece, boned side up, between 2 pieces of waxed paper. Working from the center out, pound chicken lightly with meat mallet to make cutlet about ⅛ inch thick. Repeat with remaining chicken breasts.

For sauce, in saucepan melt 3 tablespoons butter or margarine; stir in flour and chicken bouillon granules. Add water, milk, and wine all at once; cook and stir till thickened and bubbly. Set sauce aside.

In skillet cook onion in 1 tablespoon butter or margarine till tender but not brown. Stir in crab meat, mushrooms, cracker crumbs, parsley, salt, and pepper. Stir in 2 *tablespoons* of the sauce. Top each chicken piece with about ¼ *cup* of the crab mixture. Fold sides in; roll up.

Place seam side down in a 12x7½x2-inch baking dish. Pour remaining sauce over all. Bake, covered, in 350° oven about 1 hour or till chicken is tender. Uncover; sprinkle with Swiss cheese and paprika. Bake about 2 minutes longer or till cheese melts. Makes 8 servings.

Kaulibiak

1 cup finely chopped onion
1 cup finely chopped celery
1 cup finely chopped carrot
3 tablespoons butter *or*
      margarine
1 cup sliced fresh mushrooms
⅓ cup dairy sour cream
2 tablespoons lemon juice
¾ teaspoon dried dillweed
½ teaspoon salt
¼ teaspoon pepper
1 15½-ounce can salmon,
      drained and skin and bones
      removed
6 frozen patty shells, thawed
1 beaten egg
1 tablespoon water
   Sesame seeds, toasted
   Curly endive *or* parsley
      (optional)
   Lemon-Onion Sauce

In saucepan cook onion, celery, and carrot in butter or margarine till tender but not brown. Remove from heat. Add mushrooms; stir in sour cream, lemon juice, dillweed, salt, and pepper. Flake salmon and *gently* stir into vegetable mixture. On lightly floured surface stack and press 3 patty shells together; roll to 10x8 inch rectangle.

Place pastry in ungreased 15x10x1-inch shallow baking pan. Spoon salmon mixture down center of pastry. Stack and press remaining 3 patty shells together; roll to 10x8-inch rectangle. Adjust top crust over salmon mixture. Trim edges, reserving trimmings. If desired, cut decorations from reserved trimmings and arrange over loaf. Moisten edges of dough; seal with tines of fork. Combine egg and water. Brush loaf with egg mixture. Sprinkle with toasted sesame seeds. Slit top for escape of steam. Bake in 400° oven about 30 minutes or till browned. Transfer to serving platter. Garnish with curly endive or parsley, if desired. Serve with Lemon-Onion Sauce. Makes 6 servings.

Lemon-Onion Sauce: In saucepan cook ¼ cup chopped *green onion* with ¼ teaspoon dried *dillweed* in 2 tablespoons *butter or margarine* till tender. Stir in 4 teaspoons *cornstarch* and 1½ teaspoons instant *chicken bouillon granules.* Add 1½ cups *water* all at once. Cook and stir till thickened and bubbly. Add 2 teaspoons *lemon juice.* Stir half of the hot mixture into 1 slightly beaten *egg yolk;* return to remaining hot mixture in saucepan. Continue cooking till thickened, stirring constantly.

Salmon Loaf

1 15½-ounce can salmon,
drained and skin and bones
removed
2 cups soft bread crumbs
2 tablespoons sliced green onion
1 tablespoon butter *or*
margarine, melted
½ cup milk
1 slightly beaten egg

Flake salmon. In a bowl combine salmon, bread crumbs, sliced onion, butter or margarine, ½ teaspoon *salt,* and ⅛ teaspoon *pepper;* mix well. Combine milk and egg; add to salmon mixture and mix thoroughly. Shape into a loaf in a greased shallow baking pan or in a greased 7½x3½x2-inch loaf pan. Bake in 350° oven for 35 to 40 minutes. Makes 3 or 4 servings.

Tuna and Rice Wedges

¼ cup sliced green onion
¼ cup butter *or* margarine
2 cups cooked rice
1 12½-ounce can tuna, drained
and flaked
1 cup fine dry bread crumbs
⅓ cup milk
2 slightly beaten eggs
½ teaspoon dried thyme *or*
rosemary, crushed
1 medium tomato
⅓ cup shredded cheddar cheese
Snipped parsley

In medium saucepan cook onion in butter or margarine till tender but not brown; stir in cooked rice, tuna, bread crumbs, milk, eggs, and thyme or rosemary. Spread in a greased 9-inch pie plate. Bake, covered, in 350° oven for 20 to 25 minutes or till heated through. Meanwhile, cut tomato into thick slices; cut each slice into thirds. Arrange tomato wedges atop tuna mixture. Sprinkle with shredded cheese. Bake, uncovered, about 5 minutes longer or till cheese melts. Sprinkle with parsley. Makes 6 servings.

Microwave cooking directions: In nonmetal bowl combine onion and butter or margarine. Cook, covered, in counter-top microwave oven on high power about 3 minutes or till onion is tender. Stir in cooked rice, tuna, bread crumbs, milk, eggs, and thyme or rosemary. Spread in greased 9-inch nonmetal pie plate. Micro-cook, uncovered, for 9 to 11 minutes or till heated through, giving dish a half turn after 5 minutes. Meanwhile, cut tomato into thick slices; cut each slice into thirds. Arrange tomato wedges atop tuna mixture. Sprinkle with shredded cheese. Micro-cook 1 to 2 minutes longer or till cheese is melted. Sprinkle with parsley.

Tuna-Noodle Casserole

3 cups medium noodles
(4 ounces) *or* one 8-ounce
package frozen noodles
1 cup chopped celery
¼ cup chopped onion
2 tablespoons butter *or*
margarine
2 tablespoons all-purpose flour
1 11-ounce can condensed
cheddar cheese soup
¾ cup milk
1 12½-ounce can tuna, drained
and flaked
¼ cup chopped pimiento
¼ cup grated Parmesan cheese

Cook noodles according to package directions; drain and set aside. Meanwhile, in saucepan cook celery and onion in butter or margarine till tender. Stir in flour; stir in soup and milk. Cook and stir till thickened and bubbly. Stir in tuna, pimiento, and cooked noodles.

Turn mixture into a 1½-quart casserole; top with Parmesan cheese. Bake, uncovered, in 375° oven for 20 to 25 minutes or till heated through. Makes 6 servings.

Microwave cooking directions: On range top cook noodles according to package directions; drain. Meanwhile, in a 1½-quart nonmetal casserole cook celery and onion in butter or margarine, covered, in counter-top microwave oven on high power for 4 to 5 minutes or till tender, stirring twice. Stir in flour; stir in soup and milk.

Micro-cook, uncovered, for 4 to 5 minutes or till bubbly, stirring after each minute. Fold in tuna, pimiento, and cooked noodles. Micro-cook, uncovered, for 3 to 4 minutes or till hot, stirring after 2 minutes. Stir; sprinkle with Parmesan cheese.

Savor the fresh flavors of *Red Snapper with Wild Rice Stuffing* (see recipe, page 15).
It combines the delicate tang of lemon with wild rice, mushrooms, peas, onion, and pimiento.

Salmon Scallop for Two

1 7¾-ounce can salmon
½ cup finely crushed saltine
   crackers
⅓ cup milk
¼ cup thinly sliced celery
2 teaspoons lemon juice
¼ teaspoon dried dillweed
1 tablespoon butter

Drain salmon, reserving liquid. Remove skin and bones. Flake salmon. In bowl stir together flaked salmon, reserved liquid, cracker crumbs, milk, celery, lemon juice, dillweed, and dash *pepper*. Turn into a 14-ounce casserole. Dot with butter. Bake in 350° oven about 35 minutes or till heated through. Makes 2 servings.

Fiesta Salmon (pictured on page 8)

1 11-ounce can condensed
   cheddar cheese soup
½ cup milk
1 4-ounce can green chili
   peppers, rinsed, seeded,
   and chopped
1 tablespoon minced dried onion
1 15½-ounce can salmon *or* one
   12½-ounce can tuna, drained
   and broken into chunks
1½ cups coarsely broken tortilla
   chips

In a mixing bowl combine soup, milk, chili peppers, and onion. Remove skin and bones from salmon. Add salmon or tuna and 1 cup of the tortilla chips to soup mixture. Turn into four 10-ounce casseroles or one 1-quart casserole. Top with remaining chips. Bake in 375° oven till heated through (allow about 30 minutes for individual casseroles; 40 to 45 minutes for large casserole). Makes 4 servings.

Microwave cooking directions: Prepare salmon mixture as above *except* use only ⅓ *cup* milk. Turn into 1-quart non-metal casserole. Cook, uncovered, in a counter-top microwave oven on high power 9 to 10 minutes or till hot; stir mixture after 5 minutes. Top with remaining chips.

Nutty Tuna-Noodle Bake

3 cups medium noodles
2 tablespoons butter
2 tablespoons all-purpose flour
1⅓ cups milk
1 10¾-ounce can condensed
   cream of mushroom soup
¾ cup shredded American cheese
1 12½-ounce can tuna
1 8-ounce can peas and carrots
2 tablespoons chopped pimiento
½ cup chopped peanuts

Cook noodles according to package directions; drain well. Meanwhile, in saucepan melt butter; stir in flour. Add milk and soup all at once. Cook and stir till thickened and bubbly. Remove from heat; stir in cheese till melted. Drain and flake tuna. Drain peas and carrots. Stir tuna, peas and carrots, and pimiento into soup mixture. Fold noodles into soup-tuna mixture. Turn into 2-quart casserole. Sprinkle peanuts over mixture. Bake, uncovered, in 350° oven for 30 to 35 minutes or till heated through. Makes 6 servings.

Tuna with Rice for One

1 3¾-ounce can tuna, drained
   and flaked, *or* ½ cup flaked
   cooked fish
1 small cucumber, seeded and
   chopped (½ cup)
¼ cup quick-cooking rice
¼ cup water
1 teaspoon lemon juice
   Dash garlic salt
¼ cup shredded American
   cheese (1 ounce)

In a 12-ounce casserole combine tuna or ½ cup fish, cucumber, *uncooked* rice, water, lemon juice, and garlic salt. Bake, covered, in 350° oven about 25 minutes or till rice is cooked. Top with shredded cheese. Bake, uncovered, 2 to 3 minutes more or till cheese melts. Makes 1 serving.

Microwave cooking directions: In 12-ounce nonmetal casserole combine tuna, cucumber, *uncooked* rice, water, lemon juice, and garlic salt. Cook, covered with waxed paper, in a counter-top microwave oven on high power about 3 minutes. Top with cheese; micro-cook about 45 seconds.

Mushroom-Filled Fish Rolls (pictured on the cover)

4 4- to 6-ounce fresh *or* frozen
   fish fillets
3 cups fresh spinach, torn
   Water
1 cup sliced fresh mushrooms
2 tablespoons butter *or*
   margarine
1 tablespoon lemon juice
½ teaspoon dried marjoram,
   crushed
¼ teaspoon salt
⅛ teaspoon pepper
1 tablespoon butter *or*
   margarine, melted
   Bechamel Sauce

Thaw fish, if frozen; separate fillets. In covered saucepan simmer spinach with a small amount of water for 3 minutes; drain well. In saucepan cook mushrooms in 2 tablespoons butter or margarine till tender. Remove from heat; stir in cooked spinach, lemon juice, marjoram, salt, and pepper. Spoon about *3 tablespoons* mushroom mixture down center of each fillet. Roll fillet around filling; if necessary, secure with wooden picks. Place fish rolls in 8x8x2-inch baking dish. Brush tops with 1 tablespoon melted butter or margarine. Bake, uncovered, in 400° oven for 30 to 35 minutes or till fish flakes easily when tested with a fork. Remove to warmed serving platter; remove wooden picks. Top with Bechamel Sauce. Makes 4 servings.

Bechamel Sauce: In saucepan cook 2 tablespoons finely *chopped onion* in 2 tablespoons *butter or margarine* till tender but not brown. Stir in 2 teaspoons all-purpose *flour,* ¼ teaspoon *salt,* and dash *white pepper.* Add 1 cup *milk* all at once. Cook, stirring constantly, till thickened and bubbly. Stir about half the hot mixture into 2 slightly beaten *egg yolks;* return to hot mixture in saucepan. Cook and stir over low heat for 2 to 3 minutes.

Fish Sticks Polynesian (pictured on page 26)

1 8-ounce package frozen fish
   sticks
1 15½-ounce can pineapple
   chunks
1 tablespoon cornstarch
1 tablespoon soy sauce
1½ teaspoons instant chicken
   bouillon granules
2 tablespoons vinegar
1½ cups cooked rice
1 10-ounce package frozen peas,
   thawed
   Carrot curls and parsley sprigs
   (optional)

Set aside 4 fish sticks; cut remaining into 1-inch pieces. Set aside. Drain pineapple chunks, reserving ⅔ cup liquid. For sauce, in saucepan gradually stir reserved liquid into cornstarch; add soy sauce and chicken bouillon granules. Cook and stir till mixture is thickened and bubbly. Remove from heat; stir vinegar into bouillon mixture.

Combine pineapple chunks, cooked rice, peas, and fish stick pieces. Stir sauce into fish and rice mixture; turn into a 1½-quart casserole. Arrange reserved whole fish sticks atop. Bake in 350° oven for 30 to 35 minutes or till rice mixture is heated through. Garnish with carrot curls and parsley sprigs, if desired. Makes 4 servings.

Fish Florentine

1 14-ounce package frozen
   breaded fish portions
1 10-ounce package frozen
   chopped spinach
1 10-ounce package frozen
   Welsh rabbit, thawed
½ cup drained and chopped
   water chestnuts
6 slices bacon, crisp-cooked,
   drained, and crumbled
   Lemon slices (optional)

Fry fish portions according to package directions. Drain fish portions on paper toweling. Meanwhile, cook spinach according to package directions; drain.

In medium saucepan stir together spinach, Welsh rabbit, chopped water chestnuts, and bacon; heat through. Spread spinach mixture in a 10x6x2-inch baking dish. Top with fried fish portions.

Bake, uncovered, in 350° oven for about 10 minutes or till heated through. Garnish with lemon slices, if desired. Makes 6 servings.

Shrimp-Stuffed Peppers

½ cup elbow macaroni
6 large green peppers
½ cup chopped celery
3 tablespoons butter *or*
   margarine
3 tablespoons all-purpose flour
1 teaspoon seasoned salt
¼ teaspoon dried basil, crushed
1¾ cups milk
¼ teaspoon Worcestershire sauce
¾ cup shredded Swiss cheese
¼ cup dry white wine
2 4½-ounce cans shrimp,
   drained and deveined

Cook macaroni according to package directions; drain. Cut off tops of green peppers; remove seeds and membrane. Precook peppers in boiling salted water for 5 minutes; invert to drain. (For crisp peppers, omit precooking.) Cook celery in butter or margarine till tender. Stir in flour, seasoned salt, and basil. Add milk and Worcestershire sauce all at once. Cook and stir till thickened and bubbly. Add ¼ *cup* of the shredded cheese and the wine; stir till cheese melts. Stir in shrimp and macaroni.

Fill each pepper with some of the shrimp mixture; stand upright in 10x6x2-inch baking dish. Bake in 350° oven about 30 minutes. Sprinkle the remaining ½ cup shredded Swiss cheese atop peppers. Continue baking about 3 minutes more or till cheese melts. Makes 6 servings.

Scallops Tetrazzini

¾ pound fresh *or* frozen scallops
½ teaspoon minced dried onion
2 tablespoons butter
2 tablespoons all-purpose flour
½ teaspoon paprika
½ teaspoon dried oregano,
   crushed
   Few drops bottled hot pepper
   sauce
½ cup milk
1 slightly beaten egg
1 3-ounce can sliced mushrooms
4 ounces spaghetti, broken
2 tablespoons grated Parmesan
   cheese

Thaw scallops, if frozen. Cut any large scallops in half. In saucepan combine dried onion, 1 cup *water,* ¼ teaspoon *salt,* and dash *pepper.* Bring to boiling; add scallops. Return to boiling. Cover and simmer 1 minute. Drain, reserving ½ cup cooking liquid.

For sauce, melt butter in saucepan. Stir in flour, paprika, oregano, hot pepper sauce, and dash *salt.* Add the reserved ½ cup cooking liquid and the milk. Cook and stir till thickened and bubbly. Stir about half of the hot mixture into the egg. Return all to hot mixture in saucepan; mix well. Stir in *un-drained* mushrooms and scallops. Cook spaghetti according to package directions; drain. Spoon hot cooked spaghetti into a 10x6x2-inch baking dish. Top with scallop mixture; sprinkle with Parmesan cheese. Bake in 350° oven about 20 minutes. Makes 4 servings.

Curried Seafood Bake

1 cup elbow macaroni
¼ cup sliced green onion
½ teaspoon curry powder
3 tablespoons butter
3 tablespoons all-purpose flour
½ teaspoon salt
1¾ cups milk
1 cup dairy sour cream
1 5-ounce can lobster, drained,
   broken into large pieces,
   and cartilage removed, *or*
   one 7-ounce can crab meat,
   drained, flaked, and cartilage
   removed
1 4½-ounce can shrimp, drained
½ cup coarsely crushed rich
   round crackers
1 tablespoon butter, melted

Cook macaroni according to package directions; drain. Cook onion and curry in 3 tablespoons butter till onion is tender. Stir in flour and salt. Add milk; cook and stir till thickened and bubbly. Remove from heat; stir in sour cream. Gently stir in macaroni and seafood. Turn into 2-quart casserole. Mix crumbs and melted butter; sprinkle atop. Bake in 350° oven about 30 minutes. Makes 4 servings.

Microwave cooking directions: On range top cook macaroni according to package directions; drain. In 2-quart non-metal casserole cook onion and curry in 3 tablespoons butter, covered, in a counter-top microwave oven on high power about 2 minutes or till onion is tender. Stir in flour and salt; add milk. Micro-cook, uncovered, 1½ minutes; stir. Micro-cook, uncovered, 3 minutes more, stirring after every minute. Stir in sour cream; gently stir in macaroni and seafood. Micro-cook, uncovered, about 7 minutes or till heated through, stirring twice. Toss crumbs with melted butter; sprinkle atop.

Fish Provencale in tomato-mushroom sauce (see recipe, page 65), *Codfish-Cheese Open
Face Sandwiches* (see recipe, page 68), and *Seafood-Asparagus Casserole* make unusual entrées.

Seafood-Asparagus Casserole

2 10-ounce packages frozen
    asparagus spears
1 5-ounce can lobster, drained,
    broken in pieces, and
    cartilage removed
½ pound fresh *or* frozen shelled
    shrimp, cooked
3 hard-cooked eggs, sliced
2 1¾-ounce envelopes
    hollandaise sauce mix
    Milk
½ cup dairy sour cream
¾ cup soft bread crumbs
1 tablespoon grated Parmesan
    cheese
1 tablespoon butter, melted

Cook asparagus according to package directions; drain well on paper toweling. Arrange asparagus, lobster, and cooked shrimp in 10x6x2-inch baking dish. Add hard-cooked egg slices. Prepare hollandaise sauce mixes according to package directions *except* use milk for the liquid. Remove from heat. Stir in sour cream. Spoon over seafood and asparagus. Combine bread crumbs, Parmesan cheese, and melted butter; sprinkle atop. Bake in 350° oven for 20 to 25 minutes or till heated through. Makes 4 to 6 servings.

Scallop-Cheese Bake

1 pound fresh *or* frozen scallops
1 tablespoon chopped onion
3 tablespoons butter
3 tablespoons all-purpose flour
½ cup milk
1 4-ounce can chopped
    mushrooms, drained
2 tablespoons grated Parmesan
    cheese
2 tablespoons chopped pimiento
1 tablespoon snipped parsley
½ cup shredded Gruyère *or*
    Swiss cheese
½ cup finely crushed rich round
    crackers
1 tablespoon butter, melted

Thaw scallops, if frozen. Cut any large scallops in half. In saucepan cover scallops with cold water. Bring to boiling; reduce heat and simmer 1 minute. Drain, reserving ¾ *cup* of the cooking liquid.

Cook onion in 3 tablespoons butter till tender. Stir in flour and ⅛ teaspoon *pepper.* Add reserved ¾ cup cooking liquid and milk. Cook and stir till thickened and bubbly. Remove from heat. Stir in mushrooms, Parmesan cheese, pimiento, parsley, and scallops. Turn scallop mixture into 1½-quart casserole; sprinkle with Gruyère cheese. Combine crumbs and 1 tablespoon melted butter; sprinkle atop casserole. Bake in 350° oven for 20 to 25 minutes. Makes 5 or 6 servings.

Greek Shrimp Bake

1 pound fresh *or* frozen shelled
    shrimp
2 cups water
1 cup long grain rice
2 teaspoons instant chicken
    bouillon granules
1 cup bias-sliced celery
½ cup chopped onion
¼ cup butter *or* margarine
1 16-ounce can stewed
    tomatoes, cut up
¾ cup crumbled feta cheese
½ cup sliced pitted ripe olives
1 teaspoon dried dillweed

Thaw shrimp, if frozen. To prepare rice, in medium saucepan combine water, *uncooked* rice, and bouillon granules. Bring to boiling; reduce heat. Cover with tight-fitting lid. Continue cooking for 12 minutes (do not lift cover). Remove from heat; let stand, covered, 10 minutes.

In large saucepan cook celery and onion in butter or margarine till tender but not brown. Add *undrained* tomatoes; heat through. Stir in rice, *half* of the shrimp, cheese, *half* of the olives, and dillweed. Turn into 2-quart casserole. Top with remaining shrimp. Bake, uncovered, in 350° oven for 20 to 25 minutes or till shrimp are cooked. Garnish with remaining olives. Makes 6 servings.

Oysters Bienville (pictured on page 33)

20 **oysters in shells**
   Rock salt
½ **cup sliced green onion**
1 **clove garlic, minced**
2 **tablespoons butter**
2 **tablespoons all-purpose flour**
1 **teaspoon instant chicken bouillon granules**
1 **egg yolk**
⅓ **cup dry white wine**
1 **2½-ounce jar sliced mushrooms, drained**
2 **tablespoons snipped parsley**
   Dash bottled hot pepper sauce
¾ **cup soft bread crumbs**
2 **tablespoons grated Parmesan cheese**
2 **teaspoons butter, melted**

Open oysters. With knife, remove oysters. Wash shells. Place each oyster in deep half of shell. Arrange shells on bed of rock salt in shallow baking pan; set aside.

For sauce cook onion and garlic in 2 tablespoons butter till tender. Stir in flour, bouillon granules, and ¼ teaspoon *salt*. Add ⅔ cup *water;* cook and stir till mixture is thickened and bubbly. Beat egg yolk and wine together. Add about ½ cup hot mixture to egg mixture; return to hot mixture in saucepan. Stir in mushrooms, parsley, and hot pepper sauce. Cook over low heat, stirring constantly, till mixture almost boils. Toss together bread crumbs, Parmesan cheese, and 2 teaspoons melted butter.

Bake oysters in 400° oven for 5 minutes. Top each oyster with 1 tablespoon sauce. Sprinkle 1 teaspoon crumb mixture atop each. Bake 10 to 12 minutes more or till heated through. Makes 6 servings.

Scallops Mornay

½ **pound fresh *or* frozen scallops**
¾ **cup water**
½ **cup dry white wine**
¼ **teaspoon salt**
   Dash white pepper
½ **cup sliced fresh mushrooms**
2 **tablespoons chopped onion**
1 **tablespoon butter *or* margarine**
4 **teaspoons all-purpose flour**
⅓ **cup milk**
¼ **cup shredded Swiss cheese (1 ounce)**
2 **tablespoons snipped parsley**
   Hot cooked rice (optional)

Thaw scallops, if frozen. In saucepan combine water, wine, salt, and pepper; bring to boiling. Add scallops and mushrooms; return to boiling. Cover and simmer about 1 minute. Remove scallops and mushrooms; set aside. Boil the liquid, uncovered, for 10 to 15 minutes till reduced to ½ cup.

In another saucepan cook onion in butter till tender; stir in flour. Add the ½ cup scallop liquid and milk. Cook and stir till thickened and bubbly. Stir in cheese till melted. Remove from heat. Season with more salt and pepper, if desired. Stir in scallops and mushrooms. Turn into two 10-ounce casseroles. Bake, uncovered, in 375° oven for 15 to 20 minutes or till heated through. Sprinkle with parsley. Serve with hot cooked rice, if desired. Makes 2 servings.

Clams in Coquilles

1 **7½-ounce can minced clams**
¼ **cup chopped celery**
2 **tablespoons chopped onion**
1 **tablespoon butter *or* margarine**
2 **teaspoons all-purpose flour**
⅛ **teaspoon dried thyme, crushed**
   Few drops bottled hot pepper sauce
¼ **cup milk *or* clam liquid**
1 **beaten egg**
½ **cup soft bread crumbs**
2 **teaspoons snipped parsley**
2 **teaspoons butter, melted**
2 **tablespoons shredded Swiss cheese**

Drain clams; reserve ¼ cup clam liquid, if desired. In small saucepan cook celery and onion in 1 tablespoon butter till tender but not brown. Stir in flour, thyme, hot pepper sauce, ½ teaspoon *salt,* and dash *pepper.* Add milk or the reserved ¼ cup clam liquid. Cook and stir till thickened and bubbly. Stir about *half* the hot mixture into beaten egg; return to remaining hot mixture in saucepan. Stir in clams, *half* the bread crumbs, and parsley.

Spoon clam mixture into 2 buttered coquilles (individual baking shells) or 6-ounce custard cups. Toss the remaining bread crumbs with 2 teaspoons melted butter; sprinkle over clam mixture. Bake in 400° oven about 10 minutes or till browned. Sprinkle with Swiss cheese. Bake 1 minute longer or till cheese melts. Makes 2 servings.

Hot Crab Bake

¼ cup butter *or* margarine
¼ cup all-purpose flour
2 cups milk
1 7-ounce can crab meat, drained, flaked, and cartilage removed
2 hard-cooked eggs, chopped
½ cup chopped pimiento
1 teaspoon salt
⅛ teaspoon pepper
2 tablespoons butter, melted
½ cup fine dry bread crumbs
¼ cup slivered almonds

In skillet melt ¼ cup butter; stir in flour. Add milk all at once; cook and stir till thickened and bubbly. Stir in crab meat, chopped eggs, pimiento, salt, and pepper. Spoon mixture into four 10-ounce casseroles or baking shells.

Toss 2 tablespoons melted butter with bread crumbs. Sprinkle buttered crumbs atop crab mixture. Top with slivered almonds. Bake, uncovered, in 350° oven for 20 to 25 minutes or till heated through. Makes 4 servings.

Shrimp Rockefeller

2 tablespoons butter, melted
½ teaspoon celery seed
½ teaspoon Worcestershire sauce
¼ teaspoon salt
2 tablespoons sliced green onion
1 small clove garlic, minced
1 10-ounce package frozen chopped spinach, thawed
½ cup torn lettuce
½ cup light cream
1 beaten egg
¼ pound fresh *or* frozen shelled shrimp, cooked
2 tablespoons fine dry bread crumbs
2 tablespoons grated Parmesan cheese
1 tablespoon butter, melted

In medium saucepan combine 2 tablespoons butter, celery seed, Worcestershire sauce, and salt. Stir in green onion and garlic. Cook, covered, 2 to 3 minutes. Drain spinach thoroughly; stir spinach, lettuce, cream, and egg into onion mixture. Cook and stir till mixture just begins to bubble.

Divide *half* the shrimp between two 10-ounce casseroles or baking shells. Divide hot spinach mixture between casseroles; top with remaining shrimp.

Combine bread crumbs, Parmesan cheese, and 1 tablespoon melted butter; sprinkle evenly over casseroles. Bake, uncovered, in 375° oven about 15 minutes. Makes 2 servings.

Clam-Mushroom Bake

12 clams in shells, rinsed, *or* one 7½-ounce can minced clams, drained
¼ cup chopped onion
3 tablespoons butter
2 tablespoons all-purpose flour
Dash salt
Dash pepper
½ cup milk
1 2-ounce can chopped mushrooms, drained
½ cup soft bread crumbs
2 tablespoons butter, melted

If using fresh clams, open them following tip box directions on page 43. Remove edible portion and chop. Cook onion in 3 tablespoons butter till tender but not brown. Stir in flour, salt, and pepper. Add milk all at once. Cook, stirring constantly, till mixture is thickened and bubbly. Stir in fresh or canned clams and drained mushrooms. Turn into 4 baking shells. Combine bread crumbs and 2 tablespoons melted butter; sprinkle atop clam mixture. Bake in 400° oven for 10 to 15 minutes or till lightly browned. Makes 4 servings.

Introduce your friends to new combinations by making *Tuna Salad Bake,* fresh-flavored
Spanish-Style Fish (see recipe, page 10), or home-style *Fish Sticks Polynesian* (see recipe, page 20).

Coquilles Saint Jacques

1½ pounds fresh *or* frozen
    scallops
¾ cup dry white wine
1 tablespoon lemon juice
1 cup sliced fresh mushrooms
2 tablespoons thinly sliced
    green onion *or* shallots
1 clove garlic, minced
¼ cup butter *or* margarine
⅓ cup all-purpose flour
⅛ teaspoon ground nutmeg
    Dash white pepper
1 cup milk
1 cup soft bread crumbs
2 tablespoons butter *or*
    margarine, melted

Thaw scallops, if frozen. Halve any large scallops. In saucepan combine scallops, wine, lemon juice, and ½ teaspoon *salt*. Bring to boiling. Reduce heat; cover and simmer for 1 minute. Drain, reserving *1 cup* of the wine mixture (add water if necessary to make 1 cup liquid).

Cook mushrooms, green onion or shallots, and garlic in ¼ cup butter or margarine till tender. Stir in flour, nutmeg, white pepper, and ¼ teaspoon *salt*. Add milk and the reserved 1 cup wine mixture all at once. Cook and stir till thickened and bubbly. Stir in scallops; heat through. Spoon mixture into 6 buttered coquilles (baking shells), shallow individual casseroles, or 6-ounce custard cups. Toss bread crumbs with 2 tablespoons melted butter or margarine; sprinkle over scallop mixture. Bake in 400° oven about 10 minutes or till lightly browned. Makes 6 servings.

Tuna Salad Bake

1 package (8) refrigerated
    crescent rolls
1 12½-ounce can tuna, drained
    and flaked, *or* one
    15½-ounce can salmon,
    drained, flaked, and skin
    and bones removed
½ cup chopped celery
¼ cup green goddess salad
    dressing
2 cups chopped lettuce
2 medium tomatoes, chopped
4 slices American cheese,
    halved diagonally (4 ounces)

Unroll crescent roll dough; separate into 8 triangles. Place in a greased 9-inch pie plate, pressing edges together to form pie shell. Trim edges of rolls ½ inch beyond edge of pie plate; fold under. Bake, uncovered, in 350° oven about 10 minutes.

Meanwhile, combine tuna or salmon, celery, and salad dressing; spread mixture over partially baked shell. Sprinkle with chopped lettuce; top with chopped tomatoes. Bake, uncovered, for 10 minutes. Top with cheese halves; bake about 10 minutes more or till cheese melts. Makes 6 servings.

Salmon Mousse

2 egg yolks
¼ cup butter *or* margarine
¼ cup all-purpose flour
¾ teaspoon salt
⅛ teaspoon white pepper
1½ cups light cream
1 15½-ounce can salmon,
    drained, flaked, and skin and
    bones removed
1 tablespoon lemon juice
1 teaspoon finely chopped onion
4 stiff-beaten egg whites
    Egg Sauce

Beat egg yolks slightly with a fork. In saucepan melt butter or margarine; stir in flour, salt, and white pepper. Add cream all at once. Cook and stir till thickened and bubbly. Remove from heat. Stir *half* of the hot mixture into egg yolks. Return all to hot mixture in saucepan. Cook and stir 2 minutes more. Stir in salmon, lemon juice, and onion. Fold in stiff-beaten egg whites. Turn into ungreased 1½-quart soufflé dish. Bake in 325° oven for 50 to 55 minutes. Serve immediately with warm Egg Sauce. Makes 4 to 6 servings.

Egg Sauce: In saucepan cook 1 small thinly sliced *onion* in 2 tablespoons *butter or margarine* till tender; stir in 2 tablespoons all-purpose *flour*. Add 1 *bay leaf* and 1 whole *clove*. Add 1 cup *milk* all at once. Cook and stir till thickened and bubbly. Remove from heat; remove bay leaf and clove. Stir in 3 chopped *hard-cooked eggs*, 2 teaspoons drained *capers*, ¼ teaspoon *salt*, and dash white *pepper*; heat through.

Shrimp Mélange

1 **pound fresh *or* frozen shelled shrimp**
1 **9-ounce package frozen artichoke hearts**
5 **teaspoons cornstarch**
½ **teaspoon paprika**
1⅔ **cups milk**
¼ **cup dry white wine**
¾ **cup shredded Swiss cheese**
2¼ **cups cooked rice**
⅛ **teaspoon dried basil, crushed**
⅛ **teaspoon dried oregano, crushed**
Paprika
3 **tablespoons fine dry bread crumbs**
1 **tablespoon butter, melted**

Thaw shrimp, if frozen. Cook artichokes according to package directions; drain. Set aside. For cheese sauce, in medium saucepan combine cornstarch, ½ teaspoon paprika, ½ teaspoon *salt*, and dash *pepper*. Add milk all at once. Cook and stir till thickened and bubbly. Stir in wine; heat through. Stir Swiss cheese into sauce till melted. Set aside.

Combine cooked rice, basil, and oregano; turn into 1½-quart casserole. Drop shrimp into 3 cups boiling salted *water*; reduce heat and simmer for 1 to 3 minutes or till shrimp turn pink. Drain. Combine shrimp and artichokes. Top rice mixture with shrimp-artichoke mixture and cheese sauce. Sprinkle with additional paprika. Combine bread crumbs and butter or margarine; sprinkle atop casserole. Bake in 350° oven for 30 to 35 minutes. Makes 4 servings.

Lobster Quiche

Plain Pastry for Single-Crust Pie (see recipe, page 30)
3 **beaten eggs**
1½ **cups light cream *or* milk**
1 **tablespoon all-purpose flour**
1 **teaspoon Worcestershire sauce**
½ **to 1 teaspoon prepared mustard**
Dash bottled hot pepper sauce
1 **5-ounce can lobster, drained, flaked, and cartilage removed, *or* one 5½-ounce can crab meat, drained, flaked, and cartilage removed, *or* one 6½-ounce can tuna (waterpack), drained and flaked**
½ **cup shredded Swiss cheese**
½ **cup shredded Gruyère cheese**
1 **tablespoon snipped parsley**

Prepare and roll out pastry. Line a 9-inch pie plate or quiche dish with pastry. Trim pastry to ½ inch beyond edge of quiche dish or pie plate. Flute edge of pastry high; do not prick crust. Line with double thickness heavy foil. Bake in 450° oven for 5 minutes. Carefully remove foil. Bake 5 to 7 minutes more or till pastry is golden. Remove from oven; reduce oven temperature to 325°. (Pie shell should be hot when filling is added; do not partially bake pastry ahead of time.)

In bowl combine eggs, light cream or milk, flour, Worcestershire sauce, mustard, hot pepper sauce, and ¼ teaspoon *salt*. Sprinkle flaked lobster, crab, or tuna over bottom of warm pastry. Place on rack in oven. Pour egg mixture over fish or seafood. Sprinkle with Swiss and Gruyère cheeses. Top with snipped parsley. Bake in 325° oven for 45 to 50 minutes or till almost set in center. If necessary, cover edge of crust with foil to prevent overbrowning. Let stand 10 minutes before serving. Makes 6 servings.

Island Beach Clam Pie

Plain Pastry for Double-Crust Pie (see recipe, page 30)
2 **7½-ounce cans minced clams**
Milk
½ **cup chopped onion**
⅓ **cup chopped green pepper**
2 **tablespoons butter**
3 **tablespoons all-purpose flour**
¼ **teaspoon dried rosemary, crushed**
1½ **cups chopped cooked potatoes**
2 **hard-cooked eggs, chopped**

Prepare and roll out pastry. Line 9-inch pie plate with *half* the pastry. Trim even with pie plate rim. Drain clams, reserving liquid. Add enough milk to clam liquid to make 1 cup. In saucepan cook onion and green pepper in butter till tender. Stir in flour, rosemary, ½ teaspoon *salt*, and dash *pepper*. Add reserved clam liquid. Cook and stir till bubbly. Stir in clams, potatoes, and hard-cooked eggs. Spoon hot clam mixture into pastry-lined pie plate. Cut slits in second pastry circle; place atop filling. Seal and flute edge. If desired, brush with additional milk; sprinkle with toasted sesame seeds. Bake in 375° oven for 35 to 40 minutes. Let stand 10 minutes. Makes 6 servings.

Shrimp Mélange is an unusual combination of artichoke hearts, shrimp, and a rich cheese sauce. To make a meal, simply add a glass of wine and a wedge of crusty bread.

Cheesy Tuna Pies

Plain Pastry for Double-Crust
    Pie (see recipe, below)
⅓ cup sliced celery
2 tablespoons chopped onion
2 tablespoons butter *or*
    margarine
2 tablespoons all-purpose flour
¼ teaspoon salt
1 cup milk
1 9¼-ounce can tuna, drained
1 cup frozen mixed vegetables
¾ cup shredded cheddar *or*
    Swiss cheese
Milk (optional)

Prepare pastry; divide in half. Roll out *half* the pastry; cut into four 6-inch circles, rerolling if necessary. Line four 4¼x1-inch pie pans with pastry circles. Trim even with rim.

Cook celery and onion in butter or margarine till onion is tender but not brown. Stir in flour and salt. Add 1 cup milk all at once. Cook and stir till thickened and bubbly. Stir in tuna, vegetables, and cheese. Spoon hot tuna mixture into pastry-lined pie plates. Roll out remaining pastry. Cut into four 6-inch circles, rerolling if necessary. Cut slits in pastry circles for escape of steam; place atop filling. Seal and flute edges. If desired, brush tops with a little additional milk. Bake in 375° oven for 20 to 25 minutes or until crust is lightly browned. Makes 4 servings.

Note: A 9-inch pie plate may be substituted for four 4¼x1-inch pie plates. Prepare and roll out pastry. Line pie plate with *half* the pastry. Spoon in hot tuna mixture. Cut slits in second pastry circle; place atop filling. Seal; flute edge. Bake in 375° oven for 40 to 45 minutes.

Dilled Salmon Pie

Plain Pastry for Single-Crust
    Pie (see recipe, below)
2 medium onions, chopped
¼ cup chopped green pepper
2 tablespoons butter
1 tablespoon snipped parsley
¼ teaspoon dried dillweed
3 tablespoons all-purpose flour
1 cup milk
½ cup shredded Swiss cheese
1 15½-ounce can salmon,
    drained, flaked, and skin and
    bones removed
¾ cup soft bread crumbs
1 tablespoon butter, melted

Prepare and roll out pastry. Line a 9-inch pie plate; trim pastry to ½ inch beyond edge of pie plate. Flute edge; do not prick crust. Bake in 450° oven for 5 minutes. Remove from oven; reduce oven temperature to 350°.

Meanwhile, cook onion and green pepper in 2 tablespoons butter till tender. Add parsley and dillweed. Stir in flour, ½ teaspoon *salt,* and dash *pepper.* Add milk all at once; cook and stir till mixture is thickened and bubbly. Stir in cheese till melted. Gently fold in salmon. Spoon hot salmon mixture into pastry shell. Toss together bread crumbs and 1 tablespoon melted butter; sprinkle atop filling. Bake in 350° oven for 30 to 35 minutes or till lightly browned. Let stand 5 minutes before serving. Makes 6 servings.

Plain Pastry

1 cup all-purpose flour
½ teaspoon salt
⅓ cup shortening *or* lard
3 to 4 tablespoons cold water

Stir together flour and salt; cut in shortening or lard till pieces are the size of small peas. Sprinkle *1 tablespoon* of the water over part of the mixture; gently toss with a fork. Push to side of bowl. Repeat till all is moistened.

For Single-Crust Pie: Form dough into a ball. Flatten on lightly floured surface. Roll dough from center to edge, forming a circle about 12 inches in diameter. Fit pastry into a 9-inch pie plate. Trim to ½ inch beyond edge of plate. Fold under and flute edge. Continue as directed in recipe.

For Double-Crust Pie: Prepare dough as directed above *except* double the recipe. Form into 2 balls. Flatten each on lightly floured surface. Roll each from center to edge, forming a circle about 12 inches in diameter. Fit 1 circle into a 9-inch pie plate. Continue as directed in recipe.

Avocado-Sauced Tuna Crepes (pictured on page 67)

8 Yellow Cornmeal Crepes
¾ cup dairy sour cream
1 tablespoon snipped parsley
¼ teaspoon onion powder
1 9¼-ounce can tuna, drained
   and flaked
¼ cup finely chopped celery
1 6-ounce container frozen
   avocado dip, thawed
¼ cup dairy sour cream
   Dash bottled hot pepper sauce

Prepare Yellow Cornmeal Crepes; set aside. In bowl combine ¾ cup sour cream, snipped parsley, and onion powder. Fold in flaked tuna and chopped celery. Spread *3 tablespoons* tuna mixture over unbrowned side of each crepe, leaving ¼-inch rim around edge. Roll up crepes as for jelly roll. Place seam side down in 10x6x2-inch baking dish. Cover with foil. Bake in 350° oven for 20 to 25 minutes.

For sauce combine avocado dip, ¼ cup sour cream, and pepper sauce. Spoon over hot crepes. Garnish with avocado slices and watercress, if desired. Makes 4 servings.

Yellow Cornmeal Crepes: In bowl combine 3 tablespoons all-purpose *flour*, ¾ cup *milk*, ⅓ cup *yellow cornmeal*, 1 *egg*, 1½ teaspoons *cooking oil*, and ⅛ teaspoon *salt*; beat with rotary beater until blended. Heat a lightly greased 6-inch skillet; remove from heat. Spoon in about *2 tablespoons* batter; lift and tilt skillet to spread batter evenly. Return to heat; brown one side only. Invert pan over paper toweling; remove crepe. Repeat with remaining batter to make 8 crepes, greasing skillet as needed. Stir batter frequently to keep cornmeal from settling.

Salmon Filled Crepes

8 Main Dish Crepes (see recipe,
   below)
2 tablespoons butter *or*
   margarine
2 tablespoons all-purpose flour
¼ teaspoon salt
   Dash pepper
1 cup milk
1 cup shredded American cheese
1 7¾-ounce can salmon,
   drained, flaked, and skin and
   bones removed, *or* one 9¼-
   ounce can tuna, drained and
   flaked
¼ cup finely chopped celery
2 tablespoons snipped parsley
3 tablespoons milk
2 tablespoons chopped pimiento
1 tablespoon sliced almonds,
   toasted

Prepare Main Dish Crepes; set aside. In saucepan melt butter or margarine. Stir in flour, salt, and pepper. Add 1 cup milk all at once; cook and stir till thickened and bubbly. Stir in American cheese. Stir salmon or tuna, celery, and parsley into *half* of the cheese mixture. Stir 3 tablespoons milk and pimiento into the remaining cheese mixture.

Spoon salmon mixture along center of unbrowned side of crepes. Roll up crepes and place seam side down in 10x6x2-inch baking dish. Pour cheese-pimiento mixture atop. Bake in 375° oven about 20 minutes or till heated through. Garnish with toasted almonds. Let stand 5 minutes before serving. Makes 4 servings.

Main Dish Crepes

1 cup all-purpose flour
1½ cups milk
2 eggs
1 tablespoon cooking oil
¼ teaspoon salt

In bowl combine flour, milk, eggs, oil, and salt; beat with rotary beater until blended. Heat lightly greased 6-inch skillet; remove from heat. Spoon in about *2 tablespoons* batter; lift and tilt skillet to spread batter evenly. Return to heat; brown on one side only. Invert pan over paper toweling; remove crepe. Repeat with remaining batter to make 16 to 18 crepes, greasing skillet as needed.

Scallop Crepe Dinner

12 **Main Dish Crepes (see recipe, page 31)**
1½ **pounds fresh *or* frozen scallops**
4 **cups water**
2 **teaspoons salt**
1 **9-ounce package frozen Italian green beans**
3 **tablespoons butter *or* margarine**
3 **tablespoons all-purpose flour**
¾ **teaspoon salt**
¼ **teaspoon ground nutmeg Dash pepper**
1½ **cups light cream**
¼ **cup dry white wine**
⅓ **cup shredded *process* Swiss cheese**
2 **tablespoons light cream**
1 **tablespoon slivered almonds, toasted**

Prepare Main Dish Crepes; set aside. Thaw scallops, if frozen. Bring water and 2 teaspoons salt to boiling. Halve any large scallops. Add scallops to boiling water; return to boiling. Reduce heat. Cover and simmer 1 minute; drain. Cook beans according to package directions; drain. Set aside.

In saucepan melt butter or margarine. Stir in flour, ¾ teaspoon salt, nutmeg, and pepper. Add 1½ cups light cream all at once. Cook and stir till thickened and bubbly. Stir in wine. Add Swiss cheese; stir till melted. Stir in scallops and beans.

Spoon about ¼ *cup* of scallop mixture along center of unbrowned side of each crepe. Fold 2 opposite edges so they overlap atop scallop mixture. Place seam side up in 13x9x2-inch baking dish. Stir 2 tablespoons light cream into remaining scallop mixture; spoon over crepes. Cover; bake in 375° oven about 25 minutes. Sprinkle with almonds. Makes 6 servings.

Salmon Soufflé

3 **tablespoons butter**
3 **tablespoons all-purpose flour**
½ **teaspoon salt**
1 **cup milk**
3 **egg yolks**
1 **7¾-ounce can salmon, drained, flaked, and skin and bones removed, *or* one 6½-ounce can lobster, drained, flaked, and cartilage removed, *or* one 7-ounce can crab meat, drained, flaked, and cartilage removed**
1 **tablespoon finely chopped onion**
1 **tablespoon snipped parsley**
3 **egg whites Dilled Mushroom Sauce**

In saucepan melt butter; stir in flour, salt, and dash *pepper.* Add milk all at once. Cook and stir till thickened and bubbly. Remove from heat. Beat egg yolks till thick and lemon-colored. Slowly add hot mixture to egg yolks, stirring constantly. Stir in desired fish or seafood, onion, and parsley. Cool slightly. Wash beaters thoroughly. Beat egg whites till stiff peaks form; fold into fish or seafood mixture. Turn into *ungreased* 1½-quart soufflé dish. Bake in 325° oven about 45 minutes or till knife inserted near center comes out clean. Serve the soufflé immediately with Dilled Mushroom Sauce. Makes 4 servings.

Dilled Mushroom Sauce: Cook 2 tablespoons chopped *onion* in 2 tablespoons *butter or margarine* till tender but not brown. Stir in 2 tablespoons all-purpose *flour,* ½ teaspoon dried *dillweed,* ¼ teaspoon *salt,* and dash *pepper.* Add 1¼ cups *milk* all at once. Cook, stirring constantly, till mixture is thickened and bubbly. Stir in one 2½-ounce jar drained, sliced *mushrooms.*

Tuna-Rice Soufflé

1 **10¾-ounce can condensed cream of mushroom soup**
1 **6½-ounce can tuna, drained and flaked**
1 **cup *cooked* rice**
¼ **cup chopped pimiento**
2 **tablespoons snipped parsley**
4 **egg yolks**
4 **egg whites**

In saucepan heat and stir condensed soup. Stir in tuna, cooked rice, pimiento, and parsley; heat through. Beat yolks till thick and lemon-colored; slowly stir in tuna mixture. Beat egg whites till stiff peaks form. Fold tuna mixture into beaten egg whites. Turn into an *ungreased* 2-quart soufflé dish. Bake, uncovered, in 350° oven for 30 to 35 minutes or till knife inserted near center comes out clean. Serve immediately. Makes 4 servings.

Crab-Stuffed Mushrooms (see recipe, page 35), *Scallop Crepe Dinner* topped with
toasted almonds, or *Oysters Bienville* (see recipe, page 24) will add an epicurean touch to any meal.

Lobster with Fruit Stuffing

¼ cup chopped onion
2 tablespoons butter *or* margarine
1 cup peeled, sectioned, and cut up oranges
½ of an 8¼-ounce can (⅓ cup) crushed pineapple, drained
2 slices bread, toasted and cut into ¼-inch cubes
2 tablespoons snipped parsley
½ teaspoon salt
½ teaspoon dried basil, crushed
Dash pepper
2 live lobsters
¼ cup butter *or* margarine, melted
1 tablespoon cornstarch
1 tablespoon sugar
1 teaspoon instant chicken bouillon granules
⅔ cup cold water
⅓ cup dry white wine

For stuffing cook onion in 2 tablespoons butter till tender. Combine cut-up oranges and pineapple. Stir ½ *cup* fruit mixture, bread cubes, parsley, salt, basil, and pepper into onion mixture; mix well. Set aside.

Plunge live lobsters headfirst into enough boiling salted water to cover. Return to boiling; cook 20 minutes. Remove lobsters from water; place on backs on cutting board. Cut in half lengthwise, cutting to *but not through* the back shell. Draw knife from head down to base of body cavity. Discard all organs except brownish green liver and red roe (in females only). Remove black vein that runs down the tail. Crack large claws and spread body open. Stir liver and roe into stuffing.

Fill lobster cavities with stuffing. Place lobsters on baking sheet. Brush stuffed lobsters and claw meat with some of the ¼ cup melted butter. Bake the lobsters in 350° oven for 25 to 30 minutes, brushing with remaining melted butter once or twice during baking.

Meanwhile, in saucepan combine cornstarch, sugar, and bouillon granules. Stir in ⅔ cup water and wine. Cook and stir till thickened and bubbly. Stir in the remaining fruit mixture. Cover; simmer about 5 minutes. Serve with lobster. Serves 2.

Mushroom-Stuffed Lobster

2 live lobsters
⅔ cup sliced fresh mushrooms
2 tablespoons sliced green onion
1 small clove garlic, minced
6 tablespoons butter *or* margarine
1 cup soft bread crumbs
¼ cup dry sherry
¼ teaspoon salt
⅛ teaspoon pepper
2 tablespoons butter *or* margarine, melted

Plunge live lobsters headfirst into enough boiling salted water to cover. Return to boiling; cook 20 minutes. Remove lobsters from water; place on backs on cutting board. Cut in half lengthwise, cutting to *but not through* the back shell. Draw knife from head to base of body cavity. Discard all organs except brownish green liver and red roe (in females only). Remove black vein. Crack large claws. Remove meat from body; coarsely chop (leave claw meat in shell). Clean; reserve whole shells.

Cook mushrooms, green onion, and garlic in 6 tablespoons butter or margarine till tender. Reserve *2 tablespoons* bread crumbs. Stir remaining bread crumbs, sherry, salt, pepper, lobster meat, liver, and roe into mushroom mixture. Stuff shells with mixture; sprinkle with reserved bread crumbs. Place in shallow baking pan. Brush claw meat with 2 tablespoons melted butter or margarine. Bake in 350° oven for 30 to 35 minutes. Makes 2 servings.

Shrimp Cheese Turnovers

½ cup butter *or* margarine
1 3-ounce package cream cheese, cut up
1 cup all-purpose flour
½ cup cheese spread with pimiento
1 6-ounce package frozen cooked tiny shrimp, thawed

Cut butter and cream cheese into flour till mixture resembles coarse crumbs. Work with hands to form ball. Cover; chill 1 hour. On floured surface roll half into 11-inch circle; cut into rounds with 2-inch floured cutter. Spread *each* round with about ½ *teaspoon* cheese spread; top with a few shrimp. Fold in half; seal. Repeat with remaining dough, cheese, and shrimp. Bake on ungreased baking sheet in 375° oven about 15 minutes or till golden. Makes 36 appetizers.

Crab-Stuffed Mushrooms (pictured on page 33)

24 whole large fresh mushrooms
   (about 1¾-inch diameter)
1 7-ounce can crab meat,
   drained, flaked, and cartilage
   removed
1 tablespoon snipped parsley
1 teaspoon chopped capers
½ teaspoon dry mustard
¼ cup mayonnaise *or* salad
   dressing

Wash and dry mushrooms. With a sharp knife remove stems from mushrooms. (Save stems for use in another recipe.) Combine crab meat, parsley, and capers. Stir dry mustard into mayonnaise or salad dressing; toss with crab mixture. Fill *each* mushroom crown with a scant *1 tablespoon* crab mixture. Place on lightly greased baking sheet. Bake in 375° oven for 8 to 10 minutes or till heated through. Makes 24.

Microwave cooking directions: Prepare and fill mushrooms with crab mixture as above. Sprinkle with *paprika*. Arrange *12 mushrooms* on nonmetal serving plate or 9-inch pie plate. Cook, uncovered, in counter-top microwave oven on high power for 3 to 4 minutes or till heated through and mushrooms are tender. Repeat with remaining mushrooms.

Seafood Pizzas

2½ to 3 cups all-purpose flour
1 package active dry yeast
1 teaspoon salt
1 cup warm water (115° to 120°)
2 tablespoons cooking oil
½ cup chopped onion
1 clove garlic, minced
1 tablespoon cooking oil
1 15-ounce can tomato sauce
2 teaspoons dried oregano,
   crushed
½ cup sliced pitted ripe olives
2 2-ounce cans anchovy fillets,
   drained, *or* one 6-ounce
   package frozen shrimp,
   thawed
2 cups shredded mozzarella
   cheese

In large mixer bowl combine 1¼ *cups* of the flour, yeast, and salt. Add warm water and 2 tablespoons oil. Beat at low speed of electric mixer for ½ minute, scraping bowl constantly. Beat 3 minutes at high speed. Stir in as much remaining flour as you can mix in with a spoon. Turn out onto lightly floured surface. Knead in enough remaining flour to make a moderately stiff dough that is smooth and elastic (6 to 8 minutes total).

Cover dough; let rest 10 minutes. For 12-inch pizzas, divide dough in half. On lightly floured surface roll each half into a 13-inch circle. For 10-inch pizzas, divide dough into thirds; roll each third into an 11-inch circle. Transfer circles to greased 12-inch pizza pans or baking sheets. Build up edges slightly. Bake in 425° oven about 12 minutes.

In 1½-quart saucepan cook onion and garlic in 1 tablespoon cooking oil till onion is tender but not brown. Stir in tomato sauce and oregano. Cover; simmer about 10 minutes. Spread on pizza crusts. Top with sliced olives and anchovy fillets or shrimp. Sprinkle with cheese. Return to 425° oven; bake for 10 to 15 minutes longer or till bubbly. Makes two 12-inch or three 10-inch pizzas.

Seafood Pilaf

½ cup long grain rice
½ cup sliced fresh mushrooms
2 tablespoons butter *or*
   margarine
1 10½-ounce can condensed
   chicken with rice soup
1 7-ounce can crab meat,
   drained, flaked, and cartilage
   removed, *or* one 4½-ounce
   can shrimp, drained
⅓ cup dry white wine
¼ cup sliced green onion

In skillet cook rice and sliced mushrooms in butter or margarine about 4 minutes or till rice is golden brown. Remove from heat. Stir in chicken with rice soup, crab meat or shrimp, wine, and green onion. Turn into 1½-quart casserole. Bake, covered, in 350° oven for 55 minutes. Fluff the mixture with fork; bake, uncovered, about 5 minutes longer. Makes 6 side dish servings.

2 OUT OF THE SKILLET

Frying has always been one of the best ways to prepare fish and seafood. This chapter includes not only the traditional pan fried and deep-fat fried recipes, but also the popular sautéed and stir-fried recipes.

Pan-Fried Fish

3 10- to 12-ounce fresh
    or frozen pan-dressed trout
    or other fish
1 egg
2 tablespoons water
¾ cup fine dry bread crumbs *or*
    cornmeal *or* finely crushed
    saltine crackers
    (21 crackers)
½ teaspoon salt
    Dash pepper
    Shortening *or* cooking oil for
    frying

Thaw fish, if frozen. Rinse and pat dry. In a shallow dish beat egg; stir in water. In another dish combine bread crumbs, cornmeal, or crushed crackers with the salt and pepper. Dip fish in egg mixture to coat on both sides; roll fish in crumb mixture, coating evenly.

In a large skillet heat ¼ inch shortening or cooking oil. Add fish in single layer. Fry fish on one side for 4 to 5 minutes or till brown. Turn fish and fry 4 to 5 minutes longer or till both sides are brown and crisp, and fish flakes easily when tested with a fork. Drain fish on paper toweling. Makes 3 servings.

Country-Fried Catfish

1 pound fresh *or* frozen catfish
    or other fish fillets
¼ cup buttermilk *or* sour milk
½ cup all-purpose flour
1 beaten egg
¼ cup buttermilk *or* sour milk
⅓ cup all-purpose flour
⅓ cup yellow cornmeal
½ teaspoon salt
⅛ teaspoon pepper
    Shortening *or* cooking oil for
    deep-fat frying
    Lemon wedges

Thaw fish, if frozen. Cut fillets into 3x2-inch pieces. Place ¼ cup buttermilk or sour milk and ½ cup flour in separate bowls. Combine egg and remaining ¼ cup buttermilk or sour milk in another bowl. Mix ⅓ cup flour, the cornmeal, salt, and pepper in a fourth bowl. Dip fish in buttermilk, then flour, then egg mixture, and finally in cornmeal mixture to coat.

In saucepan or deep-fat fryer heat about 2 inches shortening or oil to 365°. Fry 2 or 3 fillets at a time for 5 to 7 minutes or till golden brown and fish flakes easily when tested with a fork. Drain fried fish on paper toweling; keep warm in 325° oven while frying remainder. Serve with lemon wedges. Makes 4 servings.

Clam Fritters with Creamy Wine Sauce

1 6½-ounce can minced clams
    Milk
1 cup all-purpose flour
2 teaspoons baking powder
½ teaspoon salt
1 beaten egg
    Shortening *or* cooking oil for
    deep-fat frying
    Creamy Wine Sauce

Drain clams, reserving liquid. Add enough milk to liquid to make ⅓ cup. Stir together flour, baking powder, and salt. Combine milk mixture, clams, and egg; stir into dry ingredients just till moistened.

In saucepan or deep-fat fryer heat about 2 inches shortening or oil to 365°. Carefully drop batter by tablespoonfuls into hot fat. Fry fritters 6 to 8 at a time for 2 to 3 minutes or till golden. Drain on paper toweling; keep warm in 325° oven while frying remainder. Serve immediately with Creamy Wine Sauce. Makes 6 servings.

Creamy Wine Sauce: In small saucepan melt 2 tablespoons *butter or margarine.* Blend in 2 tablespoons all-purpose *flour* and ¼ teaspoon *seasoned salt.* Add 1 cup *light cream or milk* all at once. Cook and stir till thickened and bubbly. Stir about *half* the hot mixture into 1 slightly beaten *egg yolk;* return to hot mixture in saucepan. Cook and stir 1 to 2 minutes more. Stir in ¼ cup dry white *wine* and 2 tablespoons chopped *pimiento.* Heat through.

Parmesan Fried Fish (see recipe, page 49) puts a crisp, savory coating on your favorite fish.

Scallops Amandine

1 **pound fresh *or* frozen scallops**
  Salt
  Pepper
3 **tablespoons butter *or* margarine**
¼ **cup slivered almonds**
2 **teaspoons lemon juice**
1 **tablespoon snipped parsley**
  Hot cooked rice

Thaw scallops, if frozen. Cut scallops into ½-inch-thick slices. Season scallops with salt and pepper. In large skillet melt *half* the butter or margarine. Add scallops; cook over medium-high heat about 5 minutes or till scallops are done, stirring frequently. Remove to warm platter; keep warm.

In same skillet melt remaining butter or margarine. Add almonds; toast till golden. Stir in lemon juice; pour over scallops. Sprinkle scallops with parsley; serve with hot cooked rice. Makes 4 servings.

Tempura

1 **pound fresh *or* frozen large shrimp in shells**
¾ **pound fresh *or* frozen fish steaks**
½ **pound fresh green beans**
½ **pound fresh asparagus spears**
1 **cup all-purpose flour**
2 **tablespoons cornstarch**
½ **teaspoon salt**
1 **cup ice water**
1 **egg yolk**
2 **stiffly beaten egg whites**
  Shortening *or* cooking oil for deep-fat frying
1 **teaspoon salt**
2 **medium sweet potatoes, peeled and cut into ¼-inch slices**
1 **small eggplant, peeled and cut into 1-inch cubes**
1 **cup fresh mushrooms, halved**
  Parsley sprigs
  Tempura Sauce
  Tempura Condiments

Thaw shrimp and fish steaks, if frozen. Shell and devein shrimp, referring to illustrations at right. Cut fish steaks into 1-inch pieces. Cut beans and asparagus spears into 2-inch lengths.

To make batter, stir together flour, cornstarch, and ½ teaspoon salt. Make a well in center of dry ingredients. Combine ice water and egg yolk; add all at once to dry ingredients. Slowly stir just till moistened. Do not overbeat; a few lumps should remain. Fold in egg whites; use batter at once.

In saucepan or deep-fat fryer heat about 2 inches shortening or oil to 400°. Add 1 teaspoon salt. Dip shrimp, fish, vegetables, and parsley into batter, swirling to coat. Fry, a few pieces at a time, in hot fat for 2 to 3 minutes or till golden. Drain on paper toweling. Pass Tempura Sauce and Tempura Condiments. Makes 6 to 8 servings.

Tempura Sauce: In saucepan mix 1 cup *water,* ¼ cup dry *sherry,* ¼ cup *soy sauce,* 1 teaspoon *sugar,* and 1 teaspoon instant *chicken bouillon granules.* Heat and stir till boiling.

Tempura Condiments: (1) grated *gingerroot;* (2) equal parts grated *turnip* and *radish,* mixed well; (3) ½ cup prepared *mustard* mixed with 3 tablespoons *soy sauce.*

Stuffed Fish Fillets

1½ **pounds fresh *or* frozen fish fillets**
2 **slices boiled ham**
1 **egg**
¼ **cup chopped onion**
1 **tablespoon soy sauce**
1 **teaspoon cornstarch**
1 **teaspoon grated gingerroot**
½ **teaspoon sugar**
⅛ **teaspoon pepper**
½ **cup finely chopped fresh spinach**
  Shortening *or* cooking oil for deep-fat frying

Thaw fish, if frozen. Skin fillets, if necessary. Cut fish into eight 3x2-inch pieces, patching as necessary to make even pieces. Cut ham slices into quarters.

In shallow bowl combine egg, onion, soy sauce, cornstarch, gingerroot, sugar, and pepper; mix well. Dip fish pieces into egg mixture. Place one piece of ham on each fish piece; spread *1 tablespoon* spinach over ham. Fold fish over to enclose filling; secure with wooden picks.

In saucepan or deep-fat fryer heat about 2 inches shortening or oil to 365°. Fry a few fish rolls at a time in deep hot fat for 2 to 3 minutes or till golden. Drain on paper toweling. Keep warm in 325° oven while frying remaining fish rolls. Makes 4 to 6 servings.

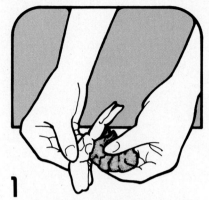

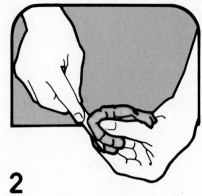

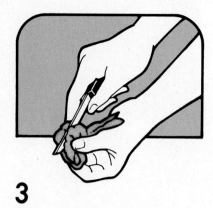

1
To shell shrimp, open the shell lengthwise down the body. Hold the shrimp in one hand and carefully peel back the shell starting with the head end. Leave the last section of the shell and tail intact. You can either cut the body portion of the shell off, leaving the tail shell in place, or you can gently pull on the tail portion of the shell and remove the entire shell.

2
Remove the sandy black vein in shrimp by making a shallow slit with a sharp knife along the back of the shrimp. Look for the vein that appears as a dark line running down the center of the back. If it is present, use the tip of the knife to scrape it out and discard it.

3
If you want to butterfly the shrimp, after removing the sandy black vein make a deeper slit in the shrimp's back. Cut almost but not all the way through the shrimp. The sides of the shrimp will open out to resemble a butterfly as shown in the illustration.

Crab-Stuffed Shrimp

24 **fresh *or* frozen large shrimp in shells**
2 **tablespoons finely chopped celery**
2 **tablespoons finely chopped green pepper**
1 **clove garlic, minced**
2 **tablespoons butter**
1 **tablespoon all-purpose flour**
¼ **cup milk**
1 **7-ounce can crab meat, drained, cartilage removed, and chopped**
½ **cup soft bread crumbs**
½ **teaspoon Worcestershire sauce**
½ **teaspoon lemon juice**
¼ **teaspoon salt**
⅛ **teaspoon pepper**
Shortening *or* cooking oil for deep-fat frying
1 **cup all-purpose flour**
½ **teaspoon sugar**
½ **teaspoon salt**
1 **slightly beaten egg**
1 **cup ice water**
2 **tablespoons cooking oil**

Thaw shrimp, if frozen. Remove shells referring to illustrations above. Butterfly shrimp by splitting down the back almost but not all the way through; remove vein. Spread shrimp open, split side up.

In saucepan cook celery, green pepper, and garlic in butter till tender; stir in 1 tablespoon flour. Add milk all at once; cook and stir till thickened and bubbly. Remove from heat. Add crab meat, bread crumbs, Worcestershire sauce, lemon juice, ¼ teaspoon salt, and pepper. Press crab mixture onto slit shrimp, packing firmly. Place on tray lined with paper toweling; chill at least 1 hour.

In saucepan or deep-fat fryer heat 2 inches shortening or oil to 360°. Meanwhile, stir together 1 cup flour, the sugar, and ½ teaspoon salt. Mix slightly beaten egg, ice water, and 2 tablespoons oil; stir into dry ingredients just till moistened (a few lumps should remain). Keep batter cool by placing the bowl in a larger bowl filled with ice cubes; use immediately.

Pat shrimp dry; dip shrimp into batter. Fry a few at a time in deep hot fat for 4 to 5 minutes or till golden. Drain on paper toweling; keep warm in 325° oven while frying remainder. Serve with lemon wedges, if desired. Makes 4 servings.

Fish can be enhanced by many flavors. A pungent sauce accents *Crispy Fried Fish with Sweet and Sour Sauce*. Elegant *Fish Fillet Newburg* (see recipe, page 63) features a wine sauce.

Crispy Fried Fish with Sweet and Sour Sauce

1 **pound fresh** *or* **frozen fish fillets**
1 **cup all-purpose flour**
½ **teaspoon sugar**
½ **teaspoon salt**
1 **beaten egg**
¾ **cup cold water**
2 **tablespoons cooking oil**
   Shortening *or* **cooking oil for deep-fat frying**
¼ **cup sugar**
2 **teaspoons cornstarch**
   Dash salt
3 **tablespoons cold water**
2 **tablespoons vinegar**
1 **tablespoon soy sauce**
1 **tablespoon dry white wine**

Thaw fish, if frozen; remove any skin. Cut fillets diagonally into 2-inch pieces; season with salt. Combine the flour, ½ teaspoon sugar, and ½ teaspoon salt. Mix the beaten egg, ¾ cup cold water, and 2 tablespoons oil; add to flour mixture. Beat till smooth.

In saucepan or deep-fat fryer heat about 2 inches shortening or oil to 375°. Dip fish pieces into batter. Fry a few pieces at a time in hot fat for 5 minutes or till golden. Drain on paper toweling; keep warm in 325° oven while frying remaining pieces.

To make sauce, in saucepan combine ¼ cup sugar, cornstarch, and dash *salt*. Stir in 3 tablespoons cold water, vinegar, soy sauce, and wine. Cook and stir till bubbly. Pass sauce with fried fish. Makes 4 servings.

Fish and Chips

1 **pound fresh** *or* **frozen fish fillets**
3 **medium potatoes (1 pound)**
   Shortening *or* **cooking oil for deep-fat frying**
½ **cup all-purpose flour**
½ **teaspoon salt**
1 **egg**
½ **cup milk**
2 **tablespoons cooking oil**
½ **cup all-purpose flour**
   Malt vinegar (optional)

Thaw fish, if frozen. Cut fillets into 3 or 4 serving-size portions. Pat dry with paper toweling. Peel potatoes; cut lengthwise into ⅜-inch-thick strips. In saucepan or deep-fat fryer heat about 2 inches shortening or cooking oil to 375°. Fry potatoes ¼ at a time for 7 to 8 minutes or till golden brown. Remove from fat; drain on paper toweling. Keep warm in 325° oven while preparing fish.

In mixing bowl stir together ½ cup flour and salt. Add egg, milk, and 2 tablespoons oil; beat till smooth. Place ½ cup flour in shallow bowl. Dip fish in flour, then in egg mixture. Fry fish in hot fat for 2 minutes on each side or till golden brown. Sprinkle fish and potatoes with salt. Sprinkle fish with vinegar, if desired. Makes 3 or 4 servings.

Fried Shrimp Balls

1½ **pounds fresh** *or* **frozen shrimp in shells**
⅓ **cup finely chopped water chestnuts**
2 **tablespoons finely chopped onion**
1 **egg**
¾ **cup soft bread crumbs (1 slice)**
2 **tablespoons finely chopped canned green chili peppers**
2 **tablespoons snipped parsley**
1 **clove garlic, minced**
½ **teaspoon salt**
¼ **teaspoon ground turmeric**
   All-purpose flour
   Shortening *or* **cooking oil for deep-fat frying**

Thaw shrimp, if frozen. Shell and devein shrimp following tip box on page 39. Pat dry with paper toweling. Cut shrimp into pieces. In small mixer bowl combine shrimp, water chestnuts, and onion; beat with electric mixer till well mashed. Add egg, bread crumbs, chili peppers, parsley, garlic, salt, and turmeric; beat well. Shape mixture into balls, using about *2 tablespoons* of the mixture for each. Roll the balls in flour to coat lightly.

In saucepan or deep-fat fryer heat about 2 inches shortening or cooking oil to 365°. Fry shrimp balls in hot fat, several at a time, for 3 minutes or till golden brown. Remove balls; drain on paper toweling. Keep warm in 325° oven while frying remainder. Makes 4 to 6 servings.

Tuna Croquettes with Cheese Sauce

3 tablespoons butter *or* margarine
¼ cup all-purpose flour
½ teaspoon instant chicken
  bouillon granules
⅔ cup milk
1 tablespoon snipped parsley
1 teaspoon lemon juice
¼ teaspoon salt
  Dash pepper
  Dash ground nutmeg
  Dash paprika
1 12½-ounce can tuna, drained
  and flaked *or* one 15½-ounce
  can salmon, drained, flaked,
  and skin and bones removed
¾ cup fine dry bread crumbs
1 beaten egg
2 tablespoons water
  Shortening *or* cooking oil for
  deep-fat frying
2 tablespoons butter *or*
  margarine
2 tablespoons all-purpose flour
¼ teaspoon salt
  Dash pepper
1¼ cups milk
½ cup shredded American cheese
½ cup shredded Swiss cheese

In saucepan melt the 3 tablespoons butter or margarine; stir in ¼ cup flour and chicken bouillon granules. Add ⅔ cup milk all at once; cook and stir till thickened and bubbly. Cook and stir 1 minute more; remove from heat. Stir in parsley, lemon juice, ¼ teaspoon salt, dash pepper, nutmeg, and paprika. Add tuna or salmon; mix well. Cover and chill for several hours.

With wet hands shape tuna mixture into 8 balls. Roll each in bread crumbs. To shape croquettes, form each ball into a cone. In shallow dish combine egg and water. Dip each croquette into egg mixture; roll again in crumbs.

In saucepan or deep-fat fryer heat about 2 inches shortening or cooking oil to 365°. Fry a few croquettes at a time in hot fat for 2½ to 3 minutes or till golden brown. Drain on paper toweling. Keep warm in 325° oven while frying remaining croquettes.

To make sauce, in saucepan melt 2 tablespoons butter or margarine. Stir in 2 tablespoons flour, ¼ teaspoon salt, and dash pepper. Add 1¼ cups milk all at once. Cook and stir till thickened and bubbly. Cook and stir 2 minutes more. Add cheeses; heat and stir till melted. Serve warm sauce over croquettes. Makes 4 servings.

Mustard-Sauced Tuna Balls (pictured on page 44)

1 beaten egg
¼ cup evaporated milk
¾ cup soft bread crumbs (1 slice)
2 tablespoons chopped pimiento
2 tablespoons finely chopped
  green pepper
1½ teaspoons Worcestershire
  sauce
¼ teaspoon salt
  Dash cayenne
1 12½-ounce can tuna, drained
  and flaked
1 beaten egg
1 tablespoon water
¾ cup finely crushed saltine
  crackers (21 crackers)
  Shortening *or* cooking oil for
  deep-fat frying
⅔ cup milk
4 teaspoons all-purpose flour
¼ teaspoon dry mustard
¼ teaspoon onion salt
  Dash pepper
⅓ cup dairy sour cream

In mixing bowl combine 1 egg and evaporated milk. Stir in bread crumbs, pimiento, green pepper, Worcestershire sauce, salt, and cayenne. Stir in tuna. Chill thoroughly; shape mixture into 8 balls.

Combine 1 egg and water. Dip tuna balls into egg mixture; roll in crushed crackers to coat. In saucepan or deep-fat fryer heat about 2 inches shortening or cooking oil to 375°. Fry tuna balls a few at a time for 3 to 5 minutes or till golden brown; drain on paper toweling. Keep warm in 325° oven while frying remainder.

To make mustard sauce, combine ⅔ cup milk, flour, mustard, onion salt, and dash pepper in a jar with a screw-top lid. Close lid and shake till well combined and smooth. In small saucepan cook and stir till thickened and bubbly. Gradually blend hot mixture into sour cream. Return to saucepan and heat through over low heat; *do not boil.* Serve sauce with tuna balls. Makes 4 servings.

Salmon Balls: Prepare recipe as directed above, *except* substitute one 15½-ounce can *salmon,* drained, flaked, and skin and bones removed, for the tuna.

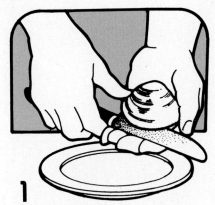

1

When opening hard-shell clams, work over a container so that all of the juice can be retained. Hold the clam in one hand with the hinged side against the palm. Using the other hand, insert a strong, thin-bladed knife between the shell halves.

2

Hold the shell firmly and run the knife blade around the opening until the muscles holding the shell together are cut. Twist the knife up slightly to pry the shell open. With your thumb pull the top half of the shell up. Be sure to keep a container under the clams to catch the juice.

3

When the shell is open, cut the hinge and cut the muscle free from the two halves of the shell. Reserve the deep half of the shell for serving "on the half shell," or put the muscle and juice in a container for use in the shucked form.

Clams Parmesan

48 **clams in shells**
1 **egg**
½ **cup finely crushed saltine crackers (14 crackers)**
½ **cup grated Parmesan cheese**
 Dash pepper
 Shortening *or* cooking oil for deep-fat frying
 Lemon wedges

Clean and open clams, referring to the illustrations above. Remove clams from shells and dry with paper toweling. Beat egg in a shallow bowl. In another bowl combine crushed crackers, Parmesan cheese, and pepper. Dip clams in beaten egg; roll in cracker mixture to coat.

In saucepan or deep-fat fryer heat about 2 inches shortening or oil to 365°. Fry clams a few at a time for 1 minute, turning once. Drain on paper toweling; keep warm in 325° oven while frying remainder. Pass lemon. Serves 4 to 6.

Codfish Balls

8 **ounces salt cod**
3 **cups diced potatoes**
⅓ **cup chopped onion**
1 **egg**
¼ **cup snipped parsley**
2 **tablespoons butter *or* margarine**
½ **teaspoon Worcestershire sauce**
¼ **teaspoon pepper**
 Shortening *or* cooking oil for deep-fat frying

Soak cod in enough water to cover for several hours or overnight, changing water several times. Drain fish; cut into small pieces. Cook cod, potatoes, and onion in boiling water for about 10 minutes or till tender; drain.

Place mixture in mixer bowl; beat with electric mixer till well combined. Add egg, parsley, butter or margarine, Worcestershire sauce, and pepper; beat well.

In saucepan or deep-fat fryer heat about 2 inches shortening or oil to 375°. Carefully drop cod mixture into hot fat by heaping tablespoonfuls. Fry 2 to 3 minutes or till balls are golden, turning once. Drain on paper toweling. Keep warm in 325° oven while frying remainder. Makes 26 to 30.

Take advantage of the versatility of tuna by making *Mustard-Sauced Tuna Balls* (see recipe, page 42). Complement the flavor of crab by making *Delaware Crab Cakes*.

Delaware Crab Cakes

1 beaten egg
½ cup finely crushed saltine
    crackers (14 crackers)
⅓ cup milk
½ teaspoon dry mustard
⅛ teaspoon white pepper
⅛ teaspoon cayenne
1 7-ounce can crab meat,
    drained, flaked, and cartilage
    removed
1 tablespoon snipped parsley
3 tablespoons shortening *or*
    cooking oil

In bowl combine egg, crushed crackers, milk, dry mustard, white pepper, and cayenne. Stir in crab meat and parsley. Using about ⅓ *cup* crab mixture for each, shape into patties. Cover and chill patties at least 30 minutes.

In skillet heat shortening or cooking oil; add patties and cook over medium heat for 6 to 8 minutes or till golden brown on both sides, turning once. Drain on paper toweling and serve immediately. Garnish with lemon wedges and parsley sprigs, if desired. Makes 5 servings.

Fried Fish Cakes

1 pound fresh *or* frozen fish
    fillets
½ cup chopped onion
5 tablespoons butter *or*
    margarine
⅓ cup fine dry bread crumbs
2 beaten eggs
⅛ teaspoon finely shredded
    lemon peel
1 tablespoon lemon juice
1 teaspoon salt
⅛ teaspoon ground ginger
    Dash pepper
¼ cup all-purpose flour
⅛ teaspoon cayenne

Thaw fish, if frozen. Steam fillets as directed on page 57. Flake fish and set aside. *(Or,* use 2 cups leftover flaked, cooked fish.) In skillet cook onion in *2 tablespoons* of the butter or margarine till tender but not brown.

Combine cooked onion, flaked fish, bread crumbs, eggs, lemon peel, lemon juice, salt, ginger, and pepper. Mix till mixture holds together. Chill 1 hour. Shape fish mixture into 8 ¾-inch-thick patties. Combine flour and cayenne. Coat fish patties with flour mixture.

In skillet melt the remaining 3 tablespoons butter or margarine. Add patties; cook over medium-low heat about 6 to 7 minutes per side or till golden brown. Makes 4 servings.

Dilled Salmon Patties

1 15½-ounce can salmon
½ cup chopped onion
2 tablespoons butter *or*
    margarine
⅔ cup fine dry bread crumbs
2 beaten eggs
1 teaspoon dried dillweed
½ teaspoon dry mustard
2 tablespoons shortening *or*
    cooking oil
2 tablespoons butter *or*
    margarine
2 tablespoons all-purpose flour
½ teaspoon salt
    Dash pepper
1 cup milk
2 beaten egg yolks
½ cup shredded American cheese
2 tablespoons lemon juice

Drain salmon, reserving ⅓ cup liquid. Remove bones and skin from salmon; flake meat. Cook onion in 2 tablespoons butter or margarine till tender but not brown. Remove from heat. Add reserved salmon liquid, ⅓ *cup* of the bread crumbs, beaten eggs, the dillweed, dry mustard, and flaked salmon; mix well. Shape into four ¾-inch-thick patties; coat with remaining bread crumbs.

In skillet heat shortening or oil. Add patties; cook over medium-low heat about 6 minutes per side or till brown.

For sauce, in saucepan melt 2 tablespoons butter or margarine; stir in flour, salt, and pepper. Add milk all at once; cook and stir till thickened and bubbly. Stir *half* the hot mixture into egg yolks. Return all to hot mixture. Stir in cheese and lemon juice till cheese is melted. Serve cheese sauce over salmon patties. Makes 4 servings.

Potato-Fish Pancakes

1 pound fresh *or* frozen fish
  fillets
2 beaten eggs
¼ cup finely chopped onion
2 tablespoons all-purpose flour
2 tablespoons snipped parsley
1 teaspoon salt
¼ teaspoon nutmeg
  Dash pepper
2 cups shredded raw potatoes
  Shortening *or* cooking oil for
  frying

Thaw fish, if frozen. Steam fish fillets according to recipe on page 57. Flake fish to make 2 cups fish. (*Or,* use 2 cups leftover flaked, cooked fish.) In mixing bowl combine eggs, onion, flour, parsley, salt, nutmeg, and pepper. Stir in flaked fish and shredded potatoes.

In skillet heat about ⅛-inch shortening or oil. For each pancake drop ⅓ cup mixture into skillet; flatten slightly with a spatula. Fry for 6 to 8 minutes or till lightly browned, turning once. Drain on paper toweling; keep warm in 325° oven while frying remaining pancakes. Serve with applesauce, if desired. Makes 6 servings.

Breakfast Clam Hash

3 medium potatoes (1 pound)
4 slices bacon
1 6½-ounce can minced clams
1 beaten egg
2 tablespoons snipped chives
½ teaspoon salt
¼ teaspoon dry mustard
  Dash pepper
¼ cup butter *or* margarine

Cook potatoes in boiling salted water till tender. Cool, peel, and shred potatoes. Cook bacon till crisp; drain and crumble. Drain the clams. In mixing bowl combine shredded potatoes, crumbled bacon, clams, egg, chives, salt, mustard, and pepper. In 10-inch skillet melt butter or margarine; remove from heat. With spatula pat potato-clam mixture into skillet, leaving a ½-inch space around edge. Cook over medium heat 6 to 8 minutes or till brown. Turn hash in large portions; brown 4 to 5 minutes longer. Makes 4 servings.

Pork and Shrimp Egg Foo Yong

½ pound boneless pork
1 tablespoon cooking oil
1 clove garlic, minced
1 cup finely chopped Chinese
  cabbage
½ cup chopped green pepper
½ cup chopped onion
1 cup water
1 teaspoon instant beef bouillon
  granules
1 teaspoon molasses
1 teaspoon soy sauce
½ teaspoon salt
¼ teaspoon sugar
2 tablespoons cold water
1 tablespoon cornstarch
6 eggs
1 teaspoon salt
¼ teaspoon pepper
1 4½-ounce can shrimp, drained
  and chopped
  Shortening *or* cooking oil for
  frying

Using cleaver or knife, chop the pork. In skillet or wok heat the 1 tablespoon oil. Stir-fry pork and garlic in the hot oil till pork is brown; drain off excess fat. Add Chinese cabbage, green pepper, and onion; stir-fry 2 to 3 minutes longer. Cool mixture.

To prepare sauce, in saucepan combine 1 cup water, beef bouillon granules, molasses, soy sauce, ½ teaspoon salt, and sugar. Bring to boiling. Stir 2 tablespoons cold water into cornstarch; stir into hot mixture. Cook and stir till thickened and bubbly. Keep warm over low heat while preparing egg foo yong.

To make egg foo yong, beat eggs, 1 teaspoon salt, and ¼ teaspoon pepper together. Stir in cooled pork-vegetable mixture. Stir in shrimp; mix well. In skillet heat about 2 tablespoons shortening or cooking oil. Using about ¼ *cup* egg mixture to make each patty, fry patties in hot fat for 1 minute on each side or till golden. (Spread meat mixture to cover egg as egg spreads slightly.) Keep warm in 325° oven while frying remaining egg patties. Repeat till all mixture is used, stirring each time; add more shortening or oil as needed. Pass sauce with egg foo yong. Makes 5 or 6 servings.

Chicken and Crab Egg Rolls

- 1 small whole chicken breast, split, skinned, and boned
- 1 tablespoon cooking oil
- 1 clove garlic, minced
- 1 cup chopped Chinese cabbage
- ½ cup finely chopped fresh *or* frozen pea pods
- ¼ cup chopped water chestnuts
- 2 tablespoons chopped onion
- ½ cup canned *or* cooked crab meat, flaked
- 1 beaten egg
- 2 tablespoons soy sauce
- 1 teaspoon dry sherry
- ¼ teaspoon salt
- ⅛ teaspoon pepper
- 6 egg roll skins
- Shortening *or* cooking oil for deep-fat frying
- Sweet and Sour Sauce

Chop chicken. In wok or skillet heat 1 tablespoon cooking oil; stir-fry chicken and garlic for 2 minutes. Add the vegetables; stir-fry 2 to 3 minutes longer. In bowl combine chicken-vegetable mixture, crab, egg, soy sauce, sherry, salt, and pepper. Cool slightly.

Wrap egg rolls as follows: Place egg roll skin with 1 point toward you. Spoon about ¼ cup filling diagonally across and just below center of skin. Fold bottom point of skin over filling; tuck point under filling. Fold side corners over, forming envelope shape. Roll up toward remaining corner; moisten point and press firmly to seal. Repeat with remaining egg roll skins and filling.

In saucepan or deep-fat fryer heat about 2 inches shortening or cooking oil to 365°. Fry egg rolls, a few at a time, in the hot fat for 2 to 3 minutes or till golden brown. Drain on paper toweling; keep warm in 325° oven. Serve with Sweet and Sour Sauce. Makes 6 egg rolls.

Sweet and Sour Sauce: In small saucepan combine ½ cup packed *brown sugar* and 1 tablespoon *cornstarch*. Stir in ⅓ cup red wine *vinegar*, ⅓ cup *chicken broth*, ¼ cup finely chopped *green pepper*, 2 tablespoons chopped *pimiento*, 1 tablespoon *soy sauce*, ¼ teaspoon *garlic powder*, and ¼ teaspoon ground *ginger*. Cook and stir over medium heat till thickened and bubbly. Serve warm. Makes 1¼ cups sauce.

Beef and Shrimp Wontons

- 1 beaten egg
- 1 cup finely chopped bok choy *or* cabbage
- ¼ cup finely chopped green onion *or* leeks
- 2 tablespoons soy sauce
- 1 tablespoon grated gingerroot
- ¼ teaspoon sugar
- ⅛ teaspoon salt
- Dash pepper
- ½ pound ground beef *or* ground pork
- 1 4½-ounce can shrimp, drained and chopped
- 40 wonton skins
- Shortening *or* cooking oil for deep-fat frying
- Horseradish-Mustard Sauce

For filling, in large mixing bowl combine egg, bok choy or cabbage, green onion or leeks, soy sauce, gingerroot, sugar, salt, and pepper. Add ground beef or pork and chopped shrimp; mix well.

Position wonton skin with one point toward you. Spoon 2 teaspoonfuls of filling just off center of skin. Fold bottom point of wonton skin over the filling; tuck point under filling. Roll once to cover filling, leaving about 1 inch unrolled at the top of the skin. Moisten the right-hand corner of skin with water. Grasp the right- and left-hand corners of skin; bring these corners toward you below the filling. Overlap the left-hand corner over the right-hand corner, then gently press the wonton skin to seal.

In saucepan or deep-fat fryer heat about 2 inches shortening or cooking oil to 365°. Fry wontons, a few at a time, in the hot fat for 2 to 3 minutes or till golden. Drain on paper toweling; keep warm in 325° oven while frying remainder. Serve warm with Horseradish-Mustard Sauce. Makes 40.

Horseradish-Mustard Sauce: In small saucepan melt 1 tablespoon *butter or margarine*. Blend in 2 tablespoons Dijon-style *mustard*, 1 tablespoon all-purpose *flour*, 1 tablespoon prepared *horseradish*, ¼ teaspoon *salt*, several drops bottled *hot pepper sauce*, and dash *pepper*. Add ½ cup *chicken broth* and ½ cup light *cream or milk*; cook and stir till thickened and bubbly. Remove from heat; stir in 2 teaspoons snipped *chives* and 1 teaspoon *lemon juice*. Serve warm. Makes 1¼ cups sauce.

Combine *French Fried Shrimp*, crispy *Deep-Fat Fried Fish*, and *Deep-Fat Fried Scallops or Oysters* to make a fish and seafood platter that includes a trio of favorites.

French-Fried Shrimp

2 pounds fresh *or* frozen shrimp in shells
1 cup all-purpose flour
½ teaspoon sugar
½ teaspoon salt
1 beaten egg
1 cup cold water
2 tablespoons cooking oil
All-purpose flour
Shortening *or* cooking oil for deep-fat frying

Thaw shrimp, if frozen. Peel shrimp, leaving last section and tail intact; devein and butterfly, referring to illustrations on page 39. Pat dry with paper toweling.

To make batter, stir together 1 cup flour, sugar, and salt. Make well in center. Combine egg, water, and 2 tablespoons oil; pour into well. Beat with rotary beater till smooth. Dip shrimp in flour to coat, then dip into batter.

In saucepan or deep-fat fryer heat about 2 inches shortening or oil to 375°. Fry a few shrimp at a time for 2 to 3 minutes or till golden. Drain on paper toweling; keep warm in 325° oven while frying remainder. Makes 6 to 8 servings.

Deep-Fat Fried Fish

1 pound fresh *or* frozen fish fillets
1 beaten egg
2 tablespoons water
¾ cup finely crushed saltine crackers *or* packaged instant mashed potato flakes
Shortening *or* cooking oil for deep-fat frying

Thaw fish, if frozen. Cut fillets into 4 serving-size pieces. Combine egg and water. In separate bowl combine crushed crackers or instant potatoes, ⅛ teaspoon *salt*, and ⅛ teaspoon *pepper*. Dip fish into egg mixture; roll in crumbs.

In saucepan or deep-fat fryer heat about 2 inches shortening or oil to 375°. Fry fish in hot fat for 3 to 5 minutes or till brown and fish flakes easily when tested with a fork. Drain on paper toweling; keep warm in 325° oven while frying remainder. Makes 4 servings.

Deep-Fat Fried Scallops or Oysters

1 pound fresh *or* frozen scallops *or* 1 pint shucked oysters
¼ cup all-purpose flour
¼ teaspoon salt
Dash pepper
1 beaten egg
1 tablespoon water
⅔ cup fine dry bread crumbs
Shortening *or* cooking oil for deep-fat frying

Thaw scallops, if frozen. Drain oysters. Dry scallops or oysters with paper toweling. Combine flour, salt, and pepper. Roll scallops or oysters in flour mixture. Combine egg and water. Dip flour-coated seafood in egg mixture; roll in bread crumbs. In saucepan or deep-fat fryer heat about 2 inches shortening or oil to 365°. Fry scallops or oysters, a few at a time, in the hot fat for 2 to 3 minutes or till golden. Drain on paper toweling; keep warm in 325° oven while frying remaining scallops or oysters. Serve with lemon or lime wedges, if desired. Makes 4 servings.

Parmesan Fried Fish (pictured on page 36)

6 8-ounce fresh *or* frozen pan-dressed fish
½ cup all-purpose flour
⅛ teaspoon garlic salt
¾ cup finely crushed saltine crackers (21 crackers)
½ cup grated Parmesan cheese
2 tablespoons snipped parsley
¼ cup milk
2 beaten eggs
3 to 4 tablespoons shortening *or* cooking oil

Thaw fish, if frozen. Dry fish with paper toweling. In shallow bowl combine flour and garlic salt; set aside. In another shallow bowl or plate combine crushed crackers, Parmesan cheese, and parsley. Place milk and eggs in separate bowls. Dip fish in milk, then in flour mixture, then in eggs, and finally in cracker mixture.

In 12-inch skillet heat shortening or oil. Add fish in a single layer. Fry over medium heat for 6 to 8 minutes or till brown on one side. Turn fish; fry 6 to 8 minutes longer or till fish flakes easily when tested with a fork. Drain fish on paper toweling. Makes 6 servings.

Tuna Stir-Fry

2 **tablespoons cornstarch**
1 **teaspoon sugar**
½ **teaspoon ground ginger**
2 **cups chicken broth**
3 **tablespoons soy sauce**
2 **tablespoons cooking oil**
3 **cups diagonally sliced bok choy** *or* **celery**
1 **clove garlic, minced**
1 **cup sliced water chestnuts**
¼ **cup sliced green onion**
2 **6½-ounce cans tuna (water pack), drained and broken into large chunks**
1 **6-ounce package frozen pea pods, thawed**
Hot cooked rice

Stir together cornstarch, sugar, and ground ginger; stir in chicken broth and soy sauce. Set aside. In large skillet or wok heat oil. Add bok choy or celery and garlic; stir-fry over high heat for 1 minute. Add water chestnuts and green onion; cook and stir 1 minute more. Stir in soy mixture; cook and stir till thickened and bubbly. Gently stir in tuna and pea pods. Cover and cook over low heat 3 to 5 minutes or till heated through. Serve over cooked rice. Makes 4 to 6 servings.

Scallop and Broccoli Stir-Fry

¾ **pound fresh** *or* **frozen scallops**
1 **10-ounce package frozen broccoli spears**
1 **8-ounce can bamboo shoots**
1 **6-ounce can whole mushrooms**
2 **tablespoons cold water**
2 **teaspoons cornstarch**
½ **cup sake** *or* **dry sherry**
1 **teaspoon sugar**
1 **teaspoon instant beef bouillon granules**
¼ **teaspoon salt**
1 **tablespoon cooking oil**
1 **medium onion, sliced**

Thaw scallops, if frozen. Thaw broccoli; halve spears cross-wise. Drain bamboo shoots and mushrooms; set aside. Mix cold water and cornstarch; stir in sake or sherry, sugar, bouillon, and salt. In large skillet or wok heat oil; stir-fry bamboo shoots, mushrooms, and onion slices in hot oil till onion is crisp-tender. Remove from wok. Add broccoli to wok; stir-fry 2 minutes. Push broccoli up sides of wok; add scallops to center of wok. Stir-fry on high heat for 3 minutes. Return all vegetables to wok; stir sake mixture and pour over all. Cook and stir till thickened and bubbly. Season to taste. Makes 3 to 4 servings.

Occidental Stir-Fry (pictured on the cover)

1 **pound fresh** *or* **frozen medium shrimp in shells**
4 **teaspoons sugar**
1 **tablespoon cornstarch**
½ **teaspoon ground ginger**
¼ **teaspoon dry mustard**
Dash pepper
¾ **cup chicken broth**
2 **tablespoons soy sauce**
1 **tablespoon lemon juice**
2 **tablespoons cooking oil**
1 **medium onion, sliced**
1 **cup bias-sliced celery**
2 **cups sliced nectarines**
Hot cooked rice

Thaw shrimp, if frozen. Shell and devein shrimp, referring to illustrations on page 39. In bowl combine sugar, cornstarch, ginger, mustard, and pepper. Stir in chicken broth, soy sauce, and lemon juice. Heat cooking oil in large skillet or wok over high heat; stir-fry onion and celery about 3 minutes or till vegetables are crisp-tender. Remove vegetables to a bowl.

If necessary add more cooking oil to skillet or wok; stir-fry shrimp for 7 to 8 minutes or till shrimp are cooked. Push shrimp away from center of wok or skillet. Stir chicken broth mixture; pour into the center of wok or skillet. Cook and stir till thickened and bubbly. Stir in vegetables, shrimp, and sliced nectarines; cover and cook about 2 minutes more or till heated through. Serve over rice. Makes 4 servings.

Here are two ways to fix canned seafood. Tuna takes on an Oriental flavor in *Tuna Stir-Fry* or combines with clams and pasta for *Skipper's Linguine* (see recipe, page 66).

Lemon Shrimp Oriental

1 **pound fresh *or* frozen shelled shrimp**
2 **tablespoons cornstarch**
1 **teaspoon sugar**
1 **teaspoon salt**
1 **teaspoon instant chicken bouillon granules**
⅛ **teaspoon pepper**
1 **cup water**
½ **teaspoon finely shredded lemon peel**
3 **tablespoons lemon juice**
2 **tablespoons cooking oil**
1 **medium green pepper, cut into strips**
1½ **cups bias-sliced celery**
¼ **cup sliced green onion**
2 **cups sliced fresh mushrooms**
1 **6-ounce package frozen pea pods**
Hot cooked rice (optional)

Thaw shrimp, if frozen. Combine cornstarch, sugar, salt, bouillon, and pepper; stir in water, lemon peel, and lemon juice. Set aside.

In large skillet or wok heat the cooking oil over high heat. Add green pepper, celery, and onion; stir-fry 3 minutes. Add mushrooms and pea pods; stir-fry 2 minutes more or till vegetables are crisp-tender. Remove vegetables; add more oil to pan, if needed. Stir-fry shrimp for 7 to 8 minutes or till done. Stir lemon mixture; add to pan. Cook and stir till thickened and bubbly. Return vegetables to pan; cover and cook 1 minute more or till heated through. Serve over rice, if desired. Makes 6 servings.

Hawaiian-Style Fish Fillets

1 **pound fresh *or* frozen fish fillets**
¼ **teaspoon salt**
Dash pepper
4 **tablespoons butter *or* margarine**
1 **small papaya, seeded, peeled, and sliced**
1 **kiwi, peeled and sliced**
¼ **cup sliced almonds**
¼ **teaspoon ground ginger**
1 **tablespoon lemon juice**

Thaw fish, if frozen. Sprinkle with salt and pepper. In skillet melt *2 tablespoons* of the butter or margarine. Cook fish fillets in butter or margarine, turning once, for 4 to 6 minutes, or till fish flakes easily when tested with a fork. Transfer fish to heated platter.

Add remaining 2 tablespoons butter or margarine to skillet. Add sliced papaya and kiwi; stir gently till heated through. Arrange the hot fruit around fish. Stir almonds and ginger into the skillet. Cook, stirring constantly, till almonds are golden brown. Stir in lemon juice; spoon over fish. Makes 4 servings.

Soy-Sauced Salmon Steaks

4 **fresh *or* frozen salmon steaks *or* other fish steaks**
Salt
2 **tablespoons cooking oil**
8 **slices lemon**
2 **tablespoons soy sauce**
1 **tablespoon mirin *or* dry sherry**
Pickled ginger *or* 1 medium cucumber, cut into strips

Thaw fish, if frozen. Sprinkle the fish steaks with salt; let stand for 10 minutes at room temperature. In a large skillet heat the cooking oil. Add fish steaks; cook about 5 minutes or till browned on one side. Turn fish and place *1* lemon slice atop *each* steak; cook fish about 5 minutes longer or till browned on other side and fish flakes easily when tested with a fork. Discard cooked lemon slices.

Combine soy sauce and mirin or dry sherry; pour over fish steaks. Cook over low heat for 1 to 2 minutes, turning steaks frequently. Remove fish to platter; pour pan juices over steaks. Top with remaining lemon slices. Garnish platter with pickled ginger or cucumber strips. Makes 4 servings.

Trout Amandine

4 to 6 pan-dressed trout (about 8 ounces each)
1 beaten egg
¼ cup light cream *or* milk
½ cup all-purpose flour
2 tablespoons cooking oil
2 tablespoons butter *or* margarine
¼ cup sliced almonds
¼ cup butter *or* margarine, melted
2 tablespoons lemon juice

Bone trout, if desired. Season trout with salt and pepper. In bowl combine egg and light cream or milk. Dip the trout in flour, then in the egg-cream mixture and again in the flour.

In large skillet, heat together oil and 2 tablespoons butter or margarine; fry trout in hot oil 5 to 6 minutes on each side or till golden and fish flakes easily when tested with a fork.

In a skillet cook almonds in the ¼ cup melted butter or margarine till almonds are golden brown. Remove from heat and stir in lemon juice. Place trout on a warm serving platter; pour almond mixture over trout and serve immediately. Makes 4 to 6 servings.

Sautéed Crab

½ pound fresh *or* frozen crab meat
2 tablespoons butter *or* margarine
1 tablespoon snipped parsley
1 teaspoon snipped chives
Dash salt
Dash pepper
Lemon wedges

Thaw crab, if frozen. Remove cartilage from crab meat; break crab into chunks. In large skillet melt butter or margarine. Add crab meat; cook, stirring constantly, on medium-high heat 3 to 4 minutes or till crab meat is heated through. Stir in parsley and chives; add salt and pepper. Serve with lemon wedges. Makes 2 servings.

Shrimp-Stuffed Mushrooms

½ cup finely shredded Chinese white radish (daikon) *or* radish
24 fresh medium mushrooms
¼ cup chopped green onion
1 tablespoon cooking oil
2 teaspoons all-purpose flour
Dash pepper
1 4½-ounce can shrimp, drained and finely chopped
⅓ cup chicken broth
3 tablespoons soy sauce
2 tablespoons mirin *or* dry sherry
½ cup all-purpose flour
1 tablespoon cornstarch
½ cup ice water
Shortening *or* cooking oil for deep-fat frying

Place shredded radish in a double layer of paper toweling; press tightly to extract as much moisture as possible. Set aside. Remove stems from mushrooms, reserving caps. Chop the stems. Cook chopped mushroom stems and green onion in the 1 tablespoon hot oil just till tender. Stir in 2 teaspoons flour and pepper. Cook and stir till thickened; stir in shrimp. Stuff mushroom caps with shrimp mixture.

To prepare dipping sauce, in saucepan combine chicken broth, soy sauce, and mirin or dry sherry; bring to boiling. Remove from heat and pour into small bowl; set aside.

For batter, stir together ½ cup flour and cornstarch. Add ice water all at once; stir just till dry ingredients are moistened. Dip stuffed mushrooms into the batter, swirling to coat evenly.

In saucepan or deep-fat fryer heat about 2 inches shortening or cooking oil to 365°. Fry mushrooms, a few at a time, in hot fat about 4 minutes or till lightly browned; turn mushrooms occasionally. Remove mushrooms; drain on paper toweling. Keep warm in 325° oven while frying the remaining mushrooms.

To serve, arrange mushrooms on a serving platter with radish mounded in the center. Dip mushrooms into sauce and eat with the shredded radish. Makes 24 appetizers.

3 ON THE RANGE

Braising, stewing, poaching, steaming, or any of the other range-top methods of cooking fish and seafood are good ways to make an entrée. Poached fish, basic boiled seafood, soups, stews, and chowders are among the recipes in this chapter.

Poached Fish with Dill Sauce

1 **3-pound fresh** *or* **frozen dressed fish**
2 **cups water**
3 **lemon slices**
1 **bay leaf**
¼ **teaspoon dried tarragon, crushed**
2 **tablespoons butter** *or* **margarine**
4 **teaspoons all-purpose flour**
2 **teaspoons lemon juice**
½ **teaspoon sugar**
½ **teaspoon dried dillweed**
1 **beaten egg yolk**

Thaw fish, if frozen. Place on large piece of cheesecloth; fold cloth over fish. Place on rack in poaching pan. Add water, lemon slices, bay leaf, tarragon, and 1 teaspoon *salt.* Cover and simmer 25 to 30 minutes or till fish flakes easily when tested with a fork. Remove from pan; keep warm. Strain and reserve 1 cup cooking liquid.

For sauce, in saucepan melt butter; stir in flour. Add reserved liquid, lemon juice, sugar, dillweed, and dash *salt.* Cook and stir till thickened and bubbly. Gradually stir ½ cup of hot mixture into egg yolk; return to hot mixture. Cook and stir 1 to 2 minutes more. Keep warm.

Pull cloth away from fish; remove and discard skin. Transfer fish to platter using 2 spatulas. Top with some sauce. Pass remaining. Makes 6 servings.

Poached Salmon with Wine Sauce

4 **fresh** *or* **frozen salmon** *or* **other fish steaks**
1¼ **cups dry white wine**
2 **tablespoons thinly sliced green onion**
2 **or 3 parsley sprigs**
1 **bay leaf**
¼ **cup whipping cream**
2 **beaten egg yolks**
½ **teaspoon lemon juice**

Thaw fish, if frozen. Place in greased 10-inch skillet. Combine wine, onion, parsley, bay leaf, ¼ teaspoon *salt,* and dash *pepper;* add to skillet. Cover and simmer 5 to 10 minutes or till fish flakes easily when tested with a fork. Remove fish and bay leaf; keep fish warm.

Boil wine mixture down to ¾ cup. Combine cream, yolks, and lemon juice; slowly stir in about *half* of the wine mixture. Return to skillet. Cook and stir over low heat till thickened and bubbly. Spoon over fish. Garnish with snipped parsley, if desired. Makes 4 servings.

Fish in Wine Sauce

1½ **pounds fresh** *or* **frozen fish steaks**
¼ **cup chopped onion**
1 **clove garlic, minced**
2 **tablespoons butter**
1 **small tomato, chopped (½ cup)**
⅓ **cup dry white wine**
1 **tablespoon snipped parsley**
½ **teaspoon salt**
   Dash pepper
⅓ **cup milk**
2 **teaspoons cornstarch**

Thaw fish, if frozen. In a 10-inch skillet cook onion and garlic in butter or margarine till tender but not brown. Add fish steaks, tomato, wine, parsley, salt, and pepper. Cover and cook over low heat for 10 to 12 minutes or till fish flakes easily when tested with a fork. Remove fish; keep warm. Stir together milk and cornstarch; add to skillet. Cook and stir till thickened and bubbly. Cook 1 to 2 minutes longer. Pour over fish. Makes 4 to 6 servings.

Microwave cooking directions: Thaw fish, if frozen. In 4-cup glass measure or bowl cook onion and garlic in butter, uncovered, in counter-top microwave oven on high power about 1½ minutes or till onion is tender. Stir in cornstarch. Stir in tomato, parsley, salt, pepper, and milk. Micro-cook, covered, about 3 minutes or till boiling, stirring twice. Stir in wine.

Place fish in 12x7½x2-inch nonmetal baking dish. Pour sauce over fish. Micro-cook, covered, 5 to 6 minutes or till fish flakes easily when tested with a fork, turning fish over after 3 minutes and spooning sauce over fish.

Poached Fish with Dill Sauce combines the fresh flavors of dill and fish.

Boiled Lobster

12 cups water*
1 tablespoon salt*
2 1- to 1½-pound live lobsters

In large kettle combine water and salt. Bring to boiling. Choose active live lobsters. Holding one lobster just behind the eyes, rinse it in cold running water. Plunge it headfirst into boiling salted water. Repeat with other lobster. Return to boiling; reduce heat and simmer over low heat for 20 minutes. Remove lobster at once.

Place each lobster on its back. With a sharp knife, cut lobster in half lengthwise. With kitchen shears or a knife, cut away the membrane on the tail. Remove black vein and body organs except red roe and liver. Crack open the large claws; break away from body. Serve in the shell with melted butter, if desired, or use in recipes as cooked lobster. Use a seafood fork to remove meat from claws, tail, and body. Pull smaller claws away from body and gently suck out the meat. Makes 2 servings or about 2 cups meat.

Note: Court bouillon is a seasoned broth often used for poaching or boiling seafood. Substitute it for water and salt when cooking lobster or other seafood.

To make court bouillon, in kettle combine 12 cups *water;* ½ cup *vinegar;* 1 *onion,* sliced; 1 *lemon,* sliced; 1 cup sliced *celery;* 1 cup sliced *carrot;* 1 tablespoon *salt;* 6 whole *cloves;* 3 whole *peppercorns;* and 3 *bay leaves.* Bring mixture to boiling; simmer, covered, for 30 minutes. When cooking smaller pieces of fish or seafood, such as scallops, strain the bouillon before cooking.

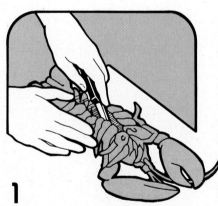

1

Cook whole, live lobsters as directed in recipe above. Place each lobster on its back on a cutting board, as shown. With a sharp knife, cut lobster in half lengthwise up to the tail section. If you are serving lobster in the shell, leave the shell back intact.

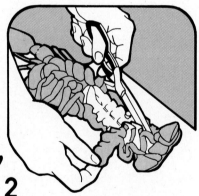

2

With kitchen shears or a sharp knife, cut away the membrane on the tail of the lobster. This step will expose the tail meat. For serving lobster in the shell, leave the meat in the tail. For use in recipes, remove the meat with a small fork and break it into lumps.

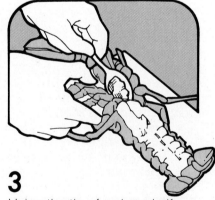

3

Using the tip of a sharp knife, scrape out the black vein that runs the length of the lobster, if present. Remove and discard the organs that are in the body cavity near the head except the red roe found only in females and the brownish-green liver known as the tomalley. Both the roe and tomalley are delicacies.

Steamed Fish

1 **pound fresh** *or* **frozen fish**
   fillets *or* **steaks** *or* **one**
   3-pound dressed fish
Water
Salt

Thaw fish, if frozen. Place a greased rack in a poacher or large skillet with a tight-fitting lid. Add water until it almost reaches rack. Bring to boiling. Sprinkle fish with salt. Place on rack; cover pan and steam till fish flakes easily when tested with a fork. Allow 3 to 4 minutes for fillets, 6 to 8 minutes for steaks, or 20 to 25 minutes for dressed fish. Carefully remove fish from pan; serve with a sauce or use in recipe as cooked fish.

Steamed Clams: Thoroughly wash 24 soft-shelled *clams* in the shells. In large kettle combine 1 gallon cold *water* and ⅓ cup *salt*. Place clams in salt-water and let stand 15 minutes. Rinse well; repeat salt-water soaking and rinsing twice. Place clams on a rack in the kettle with 1 cup hot *water.* Cover tightly and steam about 5 minutes or just till shells open. Discard any clams that do not open. Loosen clams from shells; serve with melted butter or use in a recipe as cooked clams. Makes 4 servings.

Boiled Shrimp

6 **cups water**
2 **tablespoons salt**
2 **pounds fresh** *or* **frozen shelled**
   or **unshelled shrimp**

In large saucepan combine water and salt. Bring to boiling. Add fresh or frozen shrimp. Simmer 1 to 3 minutes or till shrimp turn pink. Drain. Serve with a sauce or use in recipe as cooked shrimp. Makes 6 to 8 servings.

Boiled Scallops: Combine 4 cups *water* and 2 teaspoons *salt.* Bring to boiling. Add 2 pounds fresh *or* thawed frozen *scallops.* Simmer for 1 minute or till scallops are opaque. Drain; serve with a sauce or use in a recipe as cooked scallops. Makes 8 servings.

Boiled Frozen Lobster Tails: Heat to boiling enough *salted water* to cover lobster tails. Add frozen *lobster tails.* Simmer 3-ounce lobster tails for 3 to 4 minutes; 6-ounce lobster tails about 8 minutes; or 8-ounce lobster tails about 11 minutes. Drain; serve with butter or lemon wedges or use in a recipe as cooked lobster.

Boiled Crabs: Heat to boiling enough *salted water* to cover crabs. Plunge live, scrubbed dungeness *or* hard-shell blue *crabs* into boiling water. Simmer dungeness crabs about 8 minutes per pound; simmer blue crabs about 15 minutes in all. Drain; crack crabs according to tip box on page 72. Serve with a sauce or use in a recipe as cooked crab meat.

Boiled Crawfish: Rinse 6 pounds live *crawfish* in fresh water. In large kettle bring 3 gallons *water* and ¼ cup *salt* to boiling. Add crawfish; return to boiling and cook for 5 minutes. Drain; serve with butter or lemon wedges, or use in a recipe as cooked crawfish. Makes 4 servings.

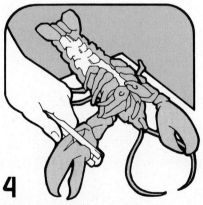

4 Use a nutcracker or lobster cracker to break open the large claws of the lobster, as shown. Break the claws away from the body and remove the meat with a seafood fork. The smaller claws may be pulled from the body and the meat gently sucked out.

Simple to prepare and spectacular to serve, *Cioppino* is a fish stew that originated on the West Coast. Serve it with loaves of sourdough bread and a favorite red or white wine.

Cioppino

1 **pound fresh** *or* **frozen fish fillets**
½ **large green pepper**
2 **tablespoons finely chopped onion**
1 **clove garlic, minced**
1 **tablespoon cooking oil**
1 **16-ounce can tomatoes, cut up**
1 **8-ounce can tomato sauce**
½ **cup dry white** *or* **red wine**
3 **tablespoons snipped parsley**
½ **teaspoon salt**
¼ **teaspoon dried oregano, crushed**
¼ **teaspoon dried basil, crushed**
  Dash pepper
2 **4½-ounce cans shrimp, drained and deveined,** *or* **12 ounces frozen shelled shrimp**
1 **6½-ounce can minced clams**

Thaw fish, if frozen. Remove any skin from fish fillets and cut fillets into 1-inch pieces; set aside. Cut green pepper into ½-inch squares.

In 3-quart saucepan cook green pepper, onion, and garlic in oil till onion is tender but not brown. Add *undrained* tomatoes, tomato sauce, wine, parsley, salt, oregano, basil, and pepper. Bring to boiling. Reduce heat; cover and simmer 20 minutes.

Add fish pieces, deveined shrimp, and *undrained* clams to tomato mixture. Bring just to boiling. Reduce heat; cover and simmer 5 to 7 minutes or till fish and shrimp are done. Makes 6 servings.

Eggplant-Zucchini Fish Stew

2 **pounds fresh** *or* **frozen fish fillets**
1 **medium onion, thinly sliced**
1 **large green pepper, chopped**
1 **clove garlic, minced**
2 **tablespoons cooking oil**
3 **cups tomato juice**
1½ **teaspoons salt**
1 **teaspoon sugar**
1 **teaspoon dried basil, crushed**
¼ **teaspoon pepper**
1 **medium eggplant**
2 **medium zucchini, sliced**
  Grated Parmesan cheese

Thaw fish, if frozen. Remove any skin from fish fillets and cut fillets into 1-inch pieces; set aside.

In 4-quart Dutch oven cook onion, green pepper, and garlic in hot cooking oil till onion is tender but not brown. Stir in tomato juice, salt, sugar, basil, and pepper. Peel and dice eggplant; add to Dutch oven. Cover and cook for 10 minutes or till eggplant is tender. Stir in zucchini and fish pieces. Cover and cook 10 to 15 minutes longer or till zucchini is tender and fish flakes easily when tested with a fork; stir occasionally.

Ladle stew into soup bowls and sprinkle each serving with Parmesan cheese. Makes 6 to 8 servings.

Salmon Bisque

½ **cup chopped onion**
½ **cup chopped celery**
2 **tablespoons butter**
3 **tablespoons all-purpose flour**
1 **teaspoon dried dillweed**
½ **teaspoon salt**
¼ **teaspoon garlic salt**
¼ **teaspoon Worcestershire sauce**
⅛ **teaspoon pepper**
4 **cups milk**
1 **7¾-ounce can salmon**
  Lemon twists

In saucepan cook onion and celery in butter till onion is tender but not brown. Stir in flour, dillweed, salt, garlic salt, Worcestershire sauce, and pepper. Add milk; cook and stir till thickened and bubbly.

Drain salmon; remove bones and skin. Flake the fish. Stir into milk mixture. Heat through; season to taste with salt and pepper. Serve with lemon twists. Makes 4 servings.

Shrimp Bisque: Prepare Salmon Bisque as directed above *except* substitute 8 ounces frozen cooked *shrimp,* thawed, for the canned salmon.

Seafood Stew

1 **pound fresh *or* frozen fish fillets**
6 **ounces frozen crab meat**
8 **clams in shells**
1 **8-ounce can whole kernel corn**
2 **cups Fish Stock *or* water**
1 **16-ounce can tomatoes, cut up**
¾ **cup dry white wine**
½ **cup chopped green pepper**
1 **medium onion, chopped (½ cup)**
2 **tablespoons snipped parsley**
1 **bay leaf**
1 **clove garlic, minced**
1 **teaspoon salt**
1 **teaspoon dried thyme, crushed**
¼ **teaspoon thread saffron, crushed**
¼ **teaspoon pepper**

Partially thaw fish and crab. Remove any skin from fish; cut fish into 1-inch pieces. Thoroughly wash clams; cover with salted water using 3 tablespoons *salt* to 8 cups cold *water.* Let stand 15 minutes; rinse. Repeat soak and rinse twice.

Drain corn. In saucepan mix corn, Fish Stock or water, *undrained* tomatoes, wine, green pepper, onion, parsley, bay leaf, garlic, salt, thyme, saffron, and pepper. Bring to boiling. Reduce heat; cover and simmer 30 minutes. Add crab, fish, and clams; cook 4 to 5 minutes or till clams open and fish flakes when tested with fork. Do not overcook. Discard bay leaf and any clams that don't open. Makes 6 to 8 servings.

Fish Stock: Cut up 1½ pounds fresh *or* frozen whole *fish* (with head and tail) to fit in large saucepan. Add 1 small *onion,* chopped; 1 stalk *celery* with leaves, chopped; 3 sprigs *parsley;* ½ *lemon,* sliced; 1 teaspoon *salt;* 3 whole black *peppercorns;* and 3 whole *cloves.* Add 6 cups cold *water.* Cover and simmer 30 minutes. Strain through sieve lined with cheesecloth. Makes 4 cups stock.

Bouillabaisse

2 **pounds fresh *or* frozen fish fillets**
1 **pound fresh *or* frozen small lobster tails**
12 **ounces fresh *or* frozen scallops**
12 **clams in shells**
2 **large onions, chopped (2 cups)**
⅓ **cup olive *or* cooking oil**
4 **cups Fish Stock (see recipe, above) *or* water**
1 **28-ounce can tomatoes, cut up**
2 **small cloves garlic, minced**
2 **sprigs parsley**
2 **bay leaves**
1 **tablespoon salt**
1½ **teaspoons dried thyme, crushed**
½ **teaspoon thread saffron, crushed**

Thaw fish and shellfish, if frozen. When lobster is partially thawed, split tails in half lengthwise; cut crosswise to make 6 to 8 portions. Cut fish fillets into 2-inch pieces. Cut large scallops in half. Wash clams well; cover with salted water using 3 tablespoons *salt* to 8 cups cold *water.* Let stand 15 minutes; rinse. Repeat soaking and rinsing twice. Set aside all seafood.

In large saucepan or Dutch oven cook onions in hot oil till tender but not brown. Add Fish Stock or water, *undrained* tomatoes, garlic, parsley, bay leaves, salt, thyme, saffron, 2 cups *water,* and ⅛ teaspoon *pepper.* Bring to boiling. Reduce heat; cover and simmer for 30 minutes. Strain liquid into a large kettle; discard vegetables and herbs.

Bring strained stock to boiling; add lobster and fish and cook 5 minutes. Add scallops and clams and boil 5 minutes longer or till clams open. Discard any clams that don't open. Serve in shallow bowls with French bread slices, if desired. Makes 6 to 8 servings.

Cauliflower-Crab Chowder

1 **10-ounce package frozen cauliflower**
2 **cups milk**
2 **tablespoons sliced green onion**
2 **tablespoons chopped pimiento**
½ **teaspoon salt**
1 **cup light cream**
3 **tablespoons all-purpose flour**
1 **7-ounce can crab meat**
1 **3-ounce package cream cheese**

In 3-quart saucepan cook cauliflower according to package directions; *do not drain.* Cut up any large pieces. Add milk, onion, pimiento, and salt. Heat and stir *just* till boiling. Combine cream and flour; add to hot milk mixture. Cook and stir till thickened and bubbly.

Drain crab; remove cartilage and cut up crab. Cube the cream cheese. Add crab and cream cheese to soup; heat and stir till cheese melts and soup is hot. Season to taste with salt and pepper. Makes 4 servings.

Seafood Stew made with fish fillets, seafood, vegetables, wine, and seasonings
is a favorite combination. It makes a special treat for family and friends on a chilly day.

New England Clam Chowder

1 **pint shucked clams, chopped**
    ***or* two 6½-ounce cans**
    minced clams
4 **ounces salt pork, diced *or* 2**
    slices bacon, cut up
4 **cups diced potatoes**
½ **cup chopped onion**
2½ **cups milk**
1 **cup light cream**
3 **tablespoons all-purpose flour**
½ **teaspoon Worcestershire sauce**

Drain clams and reserve liquid. Add enough water to liquid to measure 2 cups. In large saucepan cook pork or bacon till crisp; remove bits of pork or bacon and set aside. Add reserved clam liquid, potatoes, and onion to drippings in pan. Cover and cook about 15 minutes or till potatoes are tender. Stir in clams, *2 cups* of the milk, and the cream. Combine remaining milk and flour; stir into chowder. Cook and stir till thickened and bubbly. Cook 1 minute more. Add Worcestershire sauce, ¾ teaspoon *salt,* and dash *pepper.* Sprinkle salt pork or bacon atop. Makes 6 servings.

Manhattan Clam Chowder

1 **pint shucked clams, chopped**
    ***or* two 6½-ounce cans**
    minced clams
2 **or 3 slices bacon, cut up**
1 **cup finely chopped celery**
1 **cup chopped onion**
1 **16-ounce can tomatoes, cut up**
2 **cups diced potatoes**
½ **cup finely chopped carrot**
½ **teaspoon dried thyme, crushed**

Drain clams and reserve liquid. Add enough water to liquid to measure 3 cups liquid. In large saucepan partially cook bacon. Add celery and onion to bacon; cook till celery is tender. Stir in reserved clam liquid, *undrained* tomatoes, potatoes, carrots, thyme, 1 teaspoon *salt,* and ⅛ teaspoon *pepper.* Cover and simmer for 30 to 35 minutes or till vegetables are tender. Mash slightly with potato masher to thicken. Add clams; heat through. Makes 6 to 8 servings.

Oyster Stew

1 **pint shucked oysters**
¾ **teaspoon salt**
2 **cups milk**
1 **cup light cream**
    Dash bottled hot pepper sauce
    (optional)
    Paprika
    Butter *or* margarine

In saucepan combine oysters and their liquid and salt. Cook over medium heat for 5 minutes or till edges of oysters curl. Stir in milk, cream, and pepper sauce; heat through. Season to taste with salt and pepper. Top each serving with paprika and a pat of butter or margarine. Makes 4 servings.
Vegetable-Oyster Stew: In small saucepan cook ½ cup finely chopped *carrot* and ½ cup finely chopped *celery* in 2 tablespoons *butter or margarine,* covered, for 10 to 15 minutes or till tender. Prepare Oyster Stew as directed above; add vegetable mixture and 1 teaspoon *Worcestershire sauce* to stew. Heat through. Makes 4 servings.

Crab Fondue

1 **8-ounce package cream cheese**
1 **5-ounce jar American cheese**
    spread
1 **7-ounce can crab meat,**
    drained and flaked
2 **tablespoons milk**
2 **tablespoons dry white wine**
2 **teaspoons Worcestershire sauce**
    French bread, cubed

In saucepan over low heat melt together cheeses, stirring constantly. Remove cartilage from crab meat. Stir in crab, milk, wine, and Worcestershire. Heat through. Transfer to fondue pot; place on burner. Spear bread cubes on fondue forks; dip in fondue to coat. Makes 2¼ cups.
Microwave cooking directions: In 4-cup glass measure cook cheeses in counter-top microwave oven on high power for 2 minutes, stirring every 30 seconds. Stir in crab, milk, wine, and Worcestershire sauce. Micro-cook 3 minutes more, stirring after 1½ minutes. Serve as above.

Lobster Newburg

6 tablespoons butter *or*
    margarine
2 tablespoons all-purpose flour
1½ cups light cream
3 beaten egg yolks
1 5-ounce can (1 cup) lobster,
    broken into pieces *or* 5
    ounces frozen cooked
    lobster, thawed
3 tablespoons dry white wine
2 teaspoons lemon juice
¼ teaspoon salt
4 *or* 5 patty shells
    Paprika
    Parsley (optional)

In skillet melt butter or margarine; stir in flour. Add cream all at once. Cook and stir till thickened and bubbly. Stir *half* of hot mixture into egg yolks; return to skillet. Cook and stir till thickened, but *do not boil*. Add lobster; heat through. Stir in wine, lemon juice, and salt. Spoon into patty shells. Sprinkle with paprika; garnish with parsley, if desired. Makes 4 or 5 servings.

Crab Newburg: Prepare Lobster Newburg as directed above *except* substitute one 7-ounce can *crab meat,* drained, flaked, and cartilage removed, for the lobster.

Shrimp Newburg: Prepare Lobster Newburg as directed above *except* substitute 2 cups fresh *or* frozen cooked *shrimp* for the lobster.

Fish Fillet Newburg: Prepare Lobster Newburg as directed above *except* substitute 1 pound fresh *or* frozen *fish fillets,* steamed (see recipe, page 57) and cut up, for the lobster.

Creamed Oysters

½ cup chopped onion
½ cup chopped celery
¼ cup butter *or* margarine
1 pint shucked oysters
2 tablespoons all-purpose flour
1 teaspoon prepared mustard
1 teaspoon anchovy paste
    Dash cayenne
1 cup light cream
2 tablespoons dry sherry
4 English muffins, split

In saucepan cook onion and celery in butter or margarine till tender but not brown. Add *undrained* oysters; cook till edges of oysters curl. Stir in flour, mustard, anchovy paste, cayenne, ½ teaspoon *salt,* and ⅛ teaspoon *pepper.* Add cream; cook and stir till thickened and bubbly. Stir in sherry; heat through.

Toast English muffins; serve oysters on toasted English muffins. Makes 4 servings.

Snapper Creole

1 pound fresh *or* frozen red
    snapper *or* other fish fillets
½ cup chopped onion
½ cup chopped green pepper
1 clove garlic, minced
¼ cup butter *or* margarine
1 16-ounce can tomatoes, cut up
1 tablespoons dried parsley
    flakes
1 tablespoon instant chicken
    bouillon granules
¼ teaspoon bottled hot pepper
    sauce
1 tablespoon cornstarch
1 tablespoon cold water
    Hot cooked rice

Thaw fish, if frozen. Cut into 1-inch pieces. In 10-inch skillet cook onion, green pepper, and garlic in butter till tender. Add *undrained* tomatoes, parsley, bouillon, and hot pepper sauce. Cover and simmer 10 minutes. Combine cornstarch and water; stir into tomato mixture. Cook and stir till thickened and bubbly. Stir in fish; return to boiling. Reduce heat; cover and simmer 5 to 7 minutes or till fish flakes easily when tested with fork. Serve on rice. Makes 4 servings.

Microwave cooking directions: To thaw, place unwrapped frozen fish in nonmetal dish or pie plate. Cook in counter-top microwave oven on high power for 2 minutes, turning fish over once. Cut fish into 1-inch pieces.

In 2-quart nonmetal casserole place onion, green pepper, garlic, and butter. Micro-cook, covered, 2 minutes. Add *undrained* tomatoes, parsley, bouillon, and hot pepper sauce. Micro-cook, covered, 5 minutes. Combine cornstarch and water; stir into tomato mixture. Micro-cook, covered, 2 minutes, stirring once. Stir in fish; micro-cook, covered, 3 to 4 minutes or till done, stirring once. Serve as above.

Serve *Fish and Asparagus Bundles* next time you have guests. Wrap fish around
asparagus and chop vegetables ahead of time so you can complete preparation in about 15 minutes.

Fish and Asparagus Bundles

4 fresh *or* frozen fish fillets
¾ pound fresh asparagus *or* one
    8-ounce package frozen
    asparagus spears
1 tablespoon butter *or* margarine
2 tomatoes, peeled and cut up
½ cup sliced fresh mushrooms
¼ cup thinly sliced celery
¼ cup chopped onion
¼ cup dry white wine
1 clove garlic, minced
½ teaspoon dried mint, crushed
½ teaspoon dried basil, crushed
¼ teaspoon salt

Thaw fish, if frozen. Cut fresh asparagus into about 6-inch lengths. In covered saucepan cook fresh asparagus in small amount of boiling salted water for 8 to 10 minutes or till almost tender. (Or, cook frozen asparagus according to package directions.) Drain.

Dot fillets with butter or margarine; sprinkle with a little salt. Place asparagus across fillets; roll up fillets and fasten with wooden picks. Place fish rolls, seam side down, in 10-inch skillet. Add tomatoes, mushrooms, celery, onion, wine, garlic, mint, basil, and ¼ teaspoon salt. Cover tightly; simmer for 7 to 8 minutes or till fish flakes easily when tested with a fork. Remove fish to platter; keep warm. Boil tomato mixture gently, uncovered, for 3 minutes or till slightly thickened. Spoon over fish rolls. Makes 4 servings.

Fish Provençale (pictured on page 22)

6 fresh *or* frozen fish fillets
  Salt
  Paprika
¼ cup chopped onion
1 clove garlic, minced
1 tablespoon butter *or* margarine
½ cup dry white wine
2 tomatoes, peeled, seeded, and
    coarsely chopped *or* one
    16-ounce can tomatoes,
    drained and cut up
1 3-ounce can chopped
    mushrooms, drained
2 tablespoons snipped parsley
1 teaspoon sugar
1 teaspoon instant vegetable
    bouillon granules
2 teaspoons cornstarch
1 tablespoon cold water

Thaw fish, if frozen. Sprinkle each fillet with salt and paprika. Roll up fillets; secure with wooden picks. In 10-inch skillet cook onion and garlic in butter or margarine till onion is tender but not brown. Add wine. Stir in tomatoes, mushrooms, snipped parsley, sugar, and bouillon; bring to boiling. Add fish; reduce heat. Cover and simmer about 15 to 20 minutes or till fish flakes easily. Remove fish to platter; cover and keep warm. Boil skillet mixture, uncovered, till reduced to 1½ cups. Combine cornstarch and cold water. Add to skillet. Cook, stirring constantly, till mixture is thickened and bubbly. Spoon sauce over fish. Garnish each fish roll with a mushroom slice, if desired. Makes 6 servings.

White Clam Sauce

1 pint shucked clams *or* two 6½-
    ounce cans minced clams
¼ cup thinly sliced green onion
1 clove garlic, minced
1 tablespoon olive *or* cooking oil
¼ cup dry white wine
⅛ teaspoon white pepper
2 tablespoons snipped parsley
5 ounces hot cooked linguine,
    spaghetti, *or* other pasta

Drain shucked or canned clams, reserving ½ cup liquid. Cut up the whole clams. In saucepan cook green onion and garlic in olive or cooking oil till tender. Stir in the reserved clam liquid, the wine, and white pepper. Bring to boiling; reduce heat. Boil gently, uncovered, about 8 minutes or till liquid is reduced by about half.

Add clams and parsley. Cook and stir about 2 minutes or till clams are heated through. Toss clam mixture with pasta till coated. Serve immediately. Serve with lemon wedges, if desired. Makes 2 servings.

Shrimp Chow Mein in Crepe Cups

1½ pounds fresh *or* frozen shelled
    shrimp
¼ cup cooking oil
1 16-ounce can bean sprouts,
    drained
1 medium onion, halved and
    sliced
2 cups sliced fresh mushrooms
1 cup shredded cabbage *or* bok
    choy
1 6-ounce package frozen pea
    pods, thawed and halved
    crosswise
½ cup sliced water chestnuts
1 clove garlic, minced
1 13¾-ounce can chicken broth
¼ cup soy sauce
¼ teaspoon salt
3 tablespoons cornstarch
6 to 8 Crepe Cups
½ cup toasted slivered almonds
    Soy sauce

Thaw shrimp, if frozen; halve large shrimp lengthwise. In skillet or wok heat oil. Stir-fry shrimp in hot oil for 7 to 8 minutes; remove. Add bean sprouts, onion, mushrooms, cabbage or bok choy, pea pods, water chestnuts, and garlic to oil. Cook and stir 2 to 3 minutes. Add *1¼ cups* of the chicken broth, ¼ cup soy sauce, and salt. Cover; simmer 6 to 8 minutes. Add shrimp. Blend remaining broth into cornstarch; stir into shrimp mixture. Cook and stir till thickened and bubbly. Spoon into Crepe Cups; garnish with almonds. Pass additional soy sauce. Makes 6 to 8 servings.

Crepe Cups: Prepare Main Dish Crepes (see recipe, page 31). Invert a custard cup on a baking sheet. Grease outside of cup. Place one crepe, browned side up, atop cup. Press crepe lightly to fit cup. Repeat to make 6 to 8 cups. Bake in 375° oven 20 to 22 minutes or till crisp.

Italian Fish Portions

¼ cup chopped onion
1 clove garlic, minced
1 tablespoon cooking oil
1 tablespoon cornstarch
1 16-ounce can tomatoes, cut up
1 teaspoon dried oregano,
    crushed
½ teaspoon sugar
½ teaspoon salt
⅛ teaspoon pepper
8 frozen breaded *or* battered fish
    portions
¼ cup shredded cheddar cheese

In saucepan cook onion and garlic in oil till onion is tender but not brown. Stir in cornstarch. Stir in *undrained* tomatoes, oregano, sugar, salt, and pepper. Cook and stir till thickened and bubbly; cook and stir 2 minutes more.

Meanwhile, cook or bake fish portions according to package directions. To serve, spoon hot tomato mixture over fish. Sprinkle with shredded cheese. Makes 4 servings.

Skipper's Linguine (pictured on page 51)

6 slices bacon, cut into ½-inch
    strips
¼ cup sliced green onion
2 cloves garlic, minced
6 tablespoons butter *or*
    margarine
2 6½-ounce cans minced clams
1 6½-ounce can tuna
½ cup sliced pitted ripe olives
¼ cup snipped parsley
⅛ teaspoon pepper
12 ounces linguine

In skillet cook bacon till crisp; drain, reserving ¼ cup drippings in skillet. Set bacon aside. Cook onion and garlic in drippings till tender but not brown. Stir in butter till melted. Drain clams and tuna; break tuna into chunks. Add clams and tuna to skillet along with reserved bacon, olives, parsley, and pepper; heat through. Keep hot.

Meanwhile cook linguine according to package directions; drain. Place in warm serving bowl. At the table, top pasta with hot seafood mixture; toss. Serve with lemon wedges and grated Parmesan cheese, if desired. Makes 6 servings.

Use crepes to make your fish and seafood fancy. *Shrimp Chow Mein in Crepe Cups* and *Avocado-Sauced Tuna Crepes* (see recipe, page 31) are two examples.

Codfish-Cheese Open Face Sandwiches (pictured on page 22)

8 ounces salted cod
¼ cup butter *or* margarine
3 tablespoons all-purpose flour
½ teaspoon dry mustard
    Dash cayenne
1½ cups milk
½ teaspoon Worcestershire sauce
1 well-beaten egg
1 cup shredded American
    cheese
3 English muffins, split and
    toasted
6 tomato slices
    Parsley (optional)

Soak cod in enough water to cover for 8 to 10 hours, changing water at least once. Drain. Cook fish, covered, in enough fresh water to cover for 8 to 10 minutes or till fish flakes easily when tested with a fork. Drain and flake into small pieces. In saucepan, melt butter or margarine; stir in flour, mustard, and cayenne. Add milk and Worcestershire all at once. Cook and stir till thickened and bubbly. Gradually stir about ½ *cup* of hot mixture into beaten egg; return to mixture in pan. Cook and stir till bubbly; cook and stir 1 minute more. Stir in cheese till melted. Stir in cod; heat through. Place muffin halves on baking sheet; top each with tomato slice. Broil 3 to 4 inches from heat for 1 minute. Spoon sauce over. Garnish with parsley, if desired. Serve immediately. Makes 6 servings.

Sweet-and-Sour Fish

1 14-ounce package frozen fish
    sticks
¾ cup finely chopped green
    pepper (1 medium)
½ cup finely chopped carrot
1 clove garlic, minced
2 tablespoons cooking oil
1¾ cups water
¾ cup sugar
½ cup red wine vinegar
1 tablespoon soy sauce
1½ teaspoons instant chicken
    bouillon granules
¼ cup cold water
3 tablespoons cornstarch
    Hot cooked rice

Bake fish sticks according to package directions; cut into 1-inch pieces. Meanwhile, in a 3-quart saucepan cook green pepper, carrot, and garlic in hot oil till vegetables are tender. Add 1¾ cups water, the sugar, vinegar, soy sauce, and bouillon granules. Bring to boiling; boil rapidly for 1 minute. Mix ¼ cup cold water and the cornstarch; stir into hot mixture. Cook and stir till thickened and bubbly. Stir in fish pieces; serve over rice. Makes 4 to 6 servings.

Curried Shrimp

1 10¾-ounce can condensed
    cream of mushroom soup
¼ cup milk
3 tablespoons dry white wine
1 tablespoon sliced green onion
2 to 3 teaspoons curry powder
1 tablespoon snipped parsley
¼ teaspoon paprika
14 ounces frozen shelled shrimp
    (4 cups)
½ cup dairy sour cream
    Hot cooked rice
    Condiments (raisins, chopped
        peanuts, chutney, chopped
        tomato, chopped green
        pepper, *and/or* flaked
        coconut)

In 2-quart saucepan combine mushroom soup, milk, wine, sliced green onion, curry powder, parsley, and paprika. Bring to boiling, stirring occasionally. Stir in frozen shrimp; return to boiling. Reduce heat; cover and simmer for 5 to 10 minutes or till shrimp are tender.

Gradually stir about ½ *cup* of the hot mixture into the sour cream; return to remaining hot mixture in saucepan. Heat through but *do not boil*. Spoon curry mixture over rice; serve with any or all of the condiments. Makes 4 servings.

Curried Tuna: Prepare Curried Shrimp as directed above *except* substitute one 12½-ounce can *tuna*, drained and broken into bite-size pieces, for the shrimp.

Paella

- 12 ounces fresh *or* frozen shelled shrimp
- 12 small clams in shells
- 8 ounces chorizo *or* Italian sausage links, sliced (optional)
- 1 2½- to 3-pound broiler-fryer chicken, cut up
- 2 tablespoons olive *or* cooking oil
- 2 cups chicken broth
- 1 medium onion, cut into wedges
- 1 medium green pepper, chopped
- 1 cup long grain rice
- ½ cup chopped celery with leaves
- ¼ cup chopped pimiento
- 1 clove garlic, minced
- ½ teaspoon salt
- ½ teaspoon dried oregano, crushed
- ¼ teaspoon thread saffron, crushed
- 1 10-ounce package frozen peas

Thaw shrimp, if frozen. Cover clams in shells with salted water using 3 tablespoons *salt* to 8 cups cold *water.* Let stand 15 minutes; rinse. Repeat soaking and rinsing twice.

In 4-quart Dutch oven cook sausage 10 minutes or till done. Drain and set sausage aside. Brown chicken slowly in hot oil for 15 minutes, turning occasionally. Drain off excess fat. Add chicken broth, onion, green pepper, uncooked rice, celery, pimiento, garlic, salt, oregano, and saffron to chicken. Bring to boiling; reduce heat. Cover and simmer for 20 minutes, stirring once.

Add shrimp, clams, cooked sausage, and frozen peas. Return mixture to boiling; cover and simmer 15 minutes longer or till rice is tender and clams open; stir occasionally. Discard any clams that do not open. Makes 8 servings.

Shrimp Jambalaya

- 4 cups water
- ½ cup celery leaves
- 2 tablespoons vinegar
- 1 slice onion
- 2 teaspoons salt
- 1 teaspoon seafood seasoning
- 1½ pounds fresh *or* frozen shrimp in shells*
- ½ cup chopped onion
- ½ cup chopped celery
- 1 clove garlic, minced
- ¼ cup butter *or* margarine
- 1 16-ounce can tomatoes, cut up
- 1½ cups water
- 1 6-ounce can tomato paste
- 1 teaspoon sugar
- 1 teaspoon Worcestershire sauce
- ½ to 1 teaspoon seafood seasoning
- ¾ teaspoon salt
  Several dashes bottled hot pepper sauce
- 1 cup sliced fresh mushrooms
- 1 teaspoon filé powder
  Hot cooked rice

In large saucepan combine 4 cups water, celery leaves, vinegar, onion slice, 2 teaspoons salt, and 1 teaspoon seafood seasoning; bring to boiling. Add shrimp in shells; return to boiling. Simmer for 3 minutes or till shrimp turn pink. Drain shrimp. Peel shrimp under running water; remove vein that runs down the back. Set shrimp aside.

In large saucepan cook chopped onion, celery, and garlic in butter or margarine till tender. Add *undrained* tomatoes, 1½ cups water, tomato paste, sugar, Worcestershire sauce, ½ to 1 teaspoon seafood seasoning, ¾ teaspoon salt, and hot pepper sauce. Simmer, covered, for 30 minutes. Add cooked shrimp and mushrooms; simmer till shrimp are heated through and mushrooms are tender. Stir in filé powder; serve over hot rice. Makes 6 servings.

Note: If you use frozen shelled shrimp in Shrimp Jambalaya, use just 1 pound. Omit the first seven ingredients and do not precook the shrimp. Add shrimp along with mushrooms, and cook till shrimp are done.

4 UNDER THE BROILER

This selection of broiled, grilled, and smoked recipes will help you rediscover the delicate and delightful flavor of fish and seafood. It doesn't matter whether you are looking for an elegant dish or homestyle recipe, you can find it here.

Citrus Buttered Lobster

4 **6- to 8-ounce frozen lobster tails**
¼ **cup butter** *or* **margarine, melted**
1 **tablespoon lemon juice**
1 **teaspoon finely shredded orange peel**
¼ **teaspoon salt**
   Dash ground ginger
   Dash paprika
   Lemon wedges

Partially thaw lobster tails. Use a sharp, heavy knife to cut down through the center of the hard top shell, as shown on page 76. Cut through meat, but not through undershell. Spread tail open, butterfly-style, so lobster meat is on top. Place tails on broiler pan, shell side down. Combine melted butter, lemon juice, orange peel, salt, ginger, and paprika; brush some over lobster. Broil 4 inches from the heat 15 to 20 minutes or till meat loses its translucency and can be flaked easily when tested with a fork. Loosen meat from shell by inserting a fork between shell and meat. Brush lobster meat with butter mixture before serving. Serve with lemon wedges. Makes 4 servings.

Grilled Salmon Steaks

4 **fresh** *or* **frozen salmon** *or* **other fish steaks**
⅓ **cup cooking oil**
3 **tablespoons lemon juice**
2 **tablespoons snipped parsley**
1 **teaspoon dried dillweed**
¼ **teaspoon salt**
¼ **teaspoon dry mustard**
   Dash pepper

Thaw fish, if frozen. In shallow dish combine oil, lemon juice, parsley, dillweed, salt, dry mustard, and pepper. Add fish; let stand at room temperature for 2 hours, turning occasionally. (*Or,* marinate in refrigerator 4 to 6 hours.) Drain, reserving marinade.

Place steaks in a well-greased wire grill basket. Grill over *medium-hot* coals for 5 to 8 minutes or till lightly browned. Baste with marinade and turn; grill 5 to 8 minutes longer or till fish flakes easily when tested with a fork, basting often. Makes 4 servings.

Broiled Fillets and Steaks

2 **pounds fresh** *or* **frozen fish fillets** *or* **steaks**
2 **tablespoons butter** *or* **margarine, melted**
   Salt
   Pepper

Thaw fillets or steaks, if frozen. Cut into 6 to 8 serving-size portions. Place fish in a single layer on greased rack of broiler pan or in greased baking pan. Tuck under any thin edges. Brush *1 tablespoon* of the butter or margarine over the fish. Sprinkle with salt and pepper.

Broil fish 4 inches from the heat till fish flakes easily when tested with a fork (allow 5 to 6 minutes for each ½ inch of thickness). Brush fish with remaining butter or margarine during cooking. If more than 1 inch thick, turn when half done. Makes 6 to 8 servings.

Broiled Whole Fish: Choose one 2-pound fresh or frozen *dressed fish.* Thaw the fish, if frozen; remove head, if desired. Rinse and dry fish. Combine 3 tablespoons *butter or margarine,* melted, and 1 tablespoon *lemon juice.* Place fish on greased rack of broiler pan or in greased baking pan. Brush fish inside and out with butter mixture; sprinkle inside and out with salt and pepper.

Broil 5 inches from the heat till fish flakes easily when tested with a fork (allow 5 to 6 minutes for each ½ inch of thickness). Turn fish once during cooking; brush with remaining butter mixture. Makes 6 servings.

Ginger and orange juice complement the lobster in *Citrus Buttered Lobster.*

Citrus Fillets

- **1 pound fresh *or* frozen fish fillets**
- **½ cup water**
- **2 tablespoons frozen orange juice concentrate, thawed**
- **1 tablespoon snipped parsley**
- **1 tablespoon lemon juice**
- **1 tablespoon cooking oil**
- **½ teaspoon dried dillweed**
- **¼ teaspoon salt**
- **4 thin orange slices**

Thaw fish fillets, if frozen. Separate fillets or cut into 4 serving-size portions; place in a shallow pan. Mix water, orange juice concentrate, parsley, lemon juice, oil, dillweed, and salt; pour over fish in pan. Marinate in refrigerator 30 to 45 minutes, turning once. Remove fish, reserving marinade. Place fish on greased broiler pan. Broil fish 4 inches from the heat till fish flakes easily when tested with a fork (allow 5 minutes for each ½ inch of thickness). Baste often with marinade. If more than 1 inch thick, turn when half done. To serve, brush fish again with marinade; garnish with orange slices. Serves 4.

Scallops en Brochette

- **1 pound fresh *or* frozen scallops**
- **¼ cup Italian salad dressing**
- **¼ cup dry white wine**
- **16 fresh small mushrooms**
- **½ cup fine dry bread crumbs**
- **4 slices bacon, cut into 2-inch squares and partially cooked**
- **1 large green pepper, cut into 1-inch squares**

Thaw scallops, if frozen. Halve any large scallops. In bowl combine salad dressing and wine; add scallops and mushrooms. Cover and let stand at room temperature for 1 hour. Drain; reserve marinade.

Coat scallops with bread crumbs. On 8 skewers alternate scallops with bacon pieces, green pepper pieces, and mushrooms, ending with a mushroom. Place on grill over *medium* coals; grill 8 to 10 minutes or till scallops are tender. Turn often and baste vegetables with marinade. (Or, broil 4 inches from the heat about 10 minutes, turning once.) Serves 4.

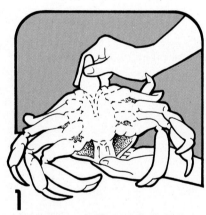

1
To crack a cooked crab, use your thumb to grasp the apron flap (the smaller portion of the shell which folds under the crab from the top shell). Pry the apron flap off by pulling up and back. Discard the apron flap; remove the top shell and discard it.

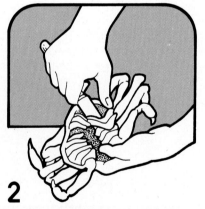

2
Using a knife edge, peel off the "devils fingers" (the long spongy substance on each side of the crab). Also remove the other internal organs in the center of the body.

With your hand firmly grasp each claw and leg of the crab. Remove the claws and legs one at a time by pulling them away from the body with a turning motion. Save them to remove any meat.

3
After the internal organs are removed, a hard, semi-transparent membrane or undershell should be exposed. The membrane or undershell covers the edible crab meat in the body cavity. To remove the meat, simply pull off the membrane and use a knife to detach the meat in large pieces.

Barbecued King Crab Legs

2 pounds frozen cooked king
  crab legs
¼ cup butter *or* margarine
¼ cup snipped parsley
¼ cup lemon juice
1 tablespoon prepared mustard
¼ teaspoon salt

Thaw crab legs and remove shells, as directed in the illustrations below. In small saucepan melt butter or margarine. Stir in snipped parsley, lemon juice, prepared mustard, and salt. Brush mixture over crab meat. Place crab meat on grill over *medium* coals. Grill 5 to 8 minutes or till crab is heated through; brush crab with butter mixture and turn occasionally. Makes 6 servings.

Broiled Salmon

2 pounds fresh *or* frozen salmon
  or other fish steaks
¼ cup cooking oil
2 tablespoons lemon juice
½ teaspoon dried rosemary,
  crushed

Thaw fish, if frozen. Cut into 6 to 8 serving-size portions. Mix oil, lemon juice, and rosemary. Let stand at room temperature 1 hour; strain. Dip fish into oil mixture; place on greased broiler pan. Sprinkle with salt and pepper. Broil 4 inches from heat till fish flakes easily when tested with fork (allow 5 minutes for each ½ inch of thickness). Turn once, brush with oil mixture. Makes 6 to 8 servings.

Broiled Oysters

36 oysters in shells
  Coarse rock salt

Open oysters in shells. With a knife remove oysters from shells and drain. Wash shells thoroughly. Place each oyster in the deep half of each shell. Arrange shells on a bed of coarse rock salt in a shallow pan. (If rock salt is unavailable steady shells on pan with crumpled foil.) Sprinkle each oyster with some table salt and pepper.

Broil oysters 4 to 5 inches from the heat for 3 to 5 minutes or till edges of oysters begin to curl. Serve with lemon wedges, if desired. Makes 6 servings.

Broiled Scallops: Choose 2 pounds fresh *or* frozen *scallops.* Thaw scallops, if frozen. Place scallops in a shallow baking pan. Sprinkle with *salt, paprika,* and *pepper.* Dot with 3 tablespoons *butter or margarine.* Broil 3 to 4 inches from the heat for 6 to 9 minutes or till scallops are lightly browned. If desired, serve with lemon wedges or tartar sauce and garnish with parsley. Makes 6 servings.

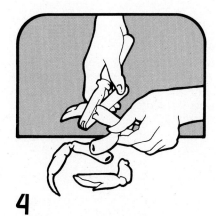

4

To crack large crab legs and claws, use a nutcracker at the joints to crack the shell. Then pick out the meat with your fingers or a nutpick. Keep the meat in the largest pieces possible. Or, expose the meat by cracking the shell with a mallet or knife handle.

Orange-Broiled Fillets

1 **pound fresh *or* frozen fish fillets**
¼ **cup orange juice**
2 **tablespoons catsup**
2 **tablespoons cooking oil**
1 **tablespoon soy sauce**
1 **tablespoon lemon juice**
¼ **teaspoon pepper**
1 **tablespoon sesame seed, toasted**

Thaw fish, if frozen. Separate fillets or cut into 4 serving-size portions. In bowl combine orange juice, catsup, cooking oil, soy sauce, lemon juice, and pepper. Pour mixture over fillets in a shallow dish. Cover and refrigerate for 2 hours. Drain fish, reserving marinade. Place fillets in greased shallow baking pan. Broil fish 4 inches from heat till fish flakes easily when tested with a fork. (Allow 5 minutes for each ½ inch of thickness.) Baste occasionally with marinade. If more than 1 inch thick, turn fish when half done. Brush again with marinade; sprinkle with sesame seed. Makes 4 servings.

Wine-Sauced Trout

6 **8-ounce fresh *or* frozen pan-dressed trout *or* other fish**
1 **15-ounce can tomato sauce**
½ **cup dry red wine**
½ **cup butter *or* margarine**
2 **tablespoons lemon juice**
2 **tablespoons sliced green onion**
1 **teaspoon sugar**
1 **teaspoon dried salad herbs**
½ **teaspoon salt**
 Few drops bottled hot pepper sauce

Thaw fish, if frozen. In small saucepan combine tomato sauce, wine, butter or margarine, lemon juice, green onion, sugar, salad herbs, salt, and hot pepper sauce. Simmer, uncovered, for 10 to 15 minutes.

Place fish on grill over *hot* coals. Grill for 10 to 12 minutes; turn and grill 10 to 12 minutes more or till fish flakes easily when tested with a fork. Brush fish with the tomato mixture during the last few minutes of grilling. Heat and pass remaining tomato mixture. If desired, garnish with green onion fans. Makes 6 servings.

Soy-Marinated Perch Fillets

2 **pounds fresh *or* frozen perch *or* other fish fillets**
⅓ **cup cooking oil**
3 **tablespoons soy sauce**
2 **tablespoons wine vinegar**
2 **tablespoons finely chopped onion**

Thaw fish, if frozen. Separate into fillets or cut into 6 to 8 serving-size portions. Place fish in plastic bag set in deep bowl. Combine oil, soy sauce, vinegar, and onion; mix well. Pour over fish; close bag. Marinate for 30 to 60 minutes at room temperature, turning bag occasionally. Drain fish, reserving marinade. Place fish in well-greased wire grill basket. Grill over *hot* coals for 8 to 9 minutes. Turn fish and brush with marinade. Grill 6 to 8 minutes more or till fish flakes easily when tested with a fork. Makes 6 to 8 servings.

Lime-Sauced Fillets with Almonds

1 **pound fresh *or* frozen fish fillets**
¼ **cup all-purpose flour**
1 **teaspoon paprika**
¼ **teaspoon salt**
4 **tablespoons butter, melted**
2 **tablespoons cooking oil**
¼ **cup slivered almonds, toasted**
2 **tablespoons lime juice**
 Several dashes bottled hot pepper sauce

Thaw fish, if frozen. Separate into fillets or cut into 4 serving-size portions. Pat dry with paper toweling. Combine flour, paprika, and salt; roll fillets in flour mixture. In 11x7x1½-inch baking pan combine 2 *tablespoons* butter and the oil. Place coated fillets in pan. Broil 4 inches from heat till fish flakes easily when tested with fork. (Allow 5 minutes for each ½ inch thickness.) Baste often with butter-oil mixture. If more than 1 inch thick, turn fish when half done. Sprinkle fish with almonds. In small saucepan mix remaining butter, lime juice, and hot pepper sauce. Stir over low heat for 1 to 2 minutes or till hot; serve with fish. Makes 4 servings.

Wine-Sauced Trout, basted in tomato-wine sauce, or *Orange-Broiled Fillets,* made
with orange marinade and topped with sesame seeds, could be the main attraction of your next meal.

Foil-Wrapped Clambake

48 **soft-shelled clams in shells**
3 **gallons cold water**
1 **cup salt**
2 **2- to 2½-pound broiler-fryer chickens, quartered**
8 **fresh ears of corn**
    Rockweed *or* parsley
8 **frozen lobster tails, thawed (about 2 pounds)**
1 **16-ounce package frozen fish fillets, thawed and cut into 8 pieces**
1 **pound butter, melted (2 cups)**

Wash clams. In kettle combine *1 gallon* water and ⅓ *cup* salt. Add clams; let stand 15 minutes. Rinse well. Repeat salt-water soaking and rinsing twice.

Break joints of chickens so they will remain flat on grill. In covered grill place chicken pieces, skin side down, over *hot* coals. Grill 10 minutes. Season with salt and pepper. Turn back husks of corn; remove silks with stiff brush. Lay husks back in place.

Tear off sixteen 36x18-inch pieces of heavy-duty foil. Place 1 sheet crosswise over a second. Repeat to make a total of 8 sets. Place a handful of rockweed or parsley on each. Cut eight 18-inch squares of cheesecloth; place each square atop rockweed. Add to each: 6 clams in shells, 1 chicken quarter, 1 ear of corn, 1 lobster tail, and 1 piece of fish. Tie ends of cheesecloth together. Seal opposite ends of foil together securely.

Place foil packages, seam side up, on grill. Close hood. Grill over *hot* coals about 45 minutes or till chicken is done and fish flakes easily when tested with a fork. Serve with individual cups of hot melted butter. Makes 8 servings.

Barbecued Rock Lobster Tails

4 **medium frozen rock lobster tails**
¼ **cup butter *or* margarine, melted**
2 **teaspoons lemon juice**
1 **teaspoon grated orange peel**
    Generous dash *each* ground ginger, aromatic bitters, and chili powder

Partially thaw rock lobster tails. Butterfly tails as directed below. Combine melted butter or margarine, lemon juice, orange peel, ginger, bitters, and chili powder; brush over lobster meat. With meat side up, grill lobster tails over *hot* coals for 5 minutes. Turn shell side up and brush with sauce. Grill 5 to 10 minutes longer or till meat loses translucency and becomes opaque. Makes 4 servings.

Butterflying Lobster Tails

For broiling and grilling, butterfly lobster tails so they will cook evenly. To do so, partially thaw frozen lobster tails. Cut through the center of hard top shell with kitchen shears or a sharp, heavy knife as shown. Cut through meat with a sharp knife, but do not cut through the undershell. Spread the meat open in the shell.

If you prefer to leave the lobster tails intact, thaw them, then cut off the thin undershell membrane with kitchen shears. Bend the tail back to crack the shell, or insert long skewers lengthwise between the shell and the meat to prevent curling.

Smoked Stuffed Salmon

1	5-pound fresh *or* frozen dressed salmon *or* other fish
	Hickory chips
½	cup finely chopped celery
¼	cup chopped onion
3	tablespoons butter *or* margarine
4	cups herb-seasoned stuffing croutons
2	tablespoons snipped parsley
½	teaspoon grated lemon peel
1	tablespoon lemon juice
¼	teaspoon salt
	Dash pepper
½	cup butter *or* margarine, melted

Thaw fish, if frozen. Soak hickory chips in enough water to cover for 1 hour before grilling. Drain chips. In saucepan cook celery and onion in the 3 tablespoons butter or margarine till tender. Pour over stuffing croutons. Add parsley, lemon peel, lemon juice, salt, and pepper. Toss together till well combined. Spoon stuffing mixture into cavity of salmon; skewer or tie closed.

In covered grill arrange *slow* coals around edge of grill. Sprinkle some dampened chips over coals. Center a foil pan on grill, not directly over coals. Place fish in foil pan. Close grill hood. Grill for 1¼ to 1½ hours or till fish flakes easily when tested with fork. Brush fish occasionally with melted butter. Sprinkle hickory chips over coals every 20 minutes. Makes 10 to 12 servings.

Pineapple-Buttered Fillets

1	pound fresh *or* frozen fish fillets
3	tablespoons butter *or* margarine, melted
1	8¼-ounce can pineapple chunks
¼	cup butter *or* margarine
1	tablespoon snipped parsley

Thaw fish, if frozen. Separate into fillets or cut into 4 serving-size portions. Place in greased baking pan. Brush with 3 tablespoons butter. Sprinkle with salt and pepper. Broil 4 inches from heat till fish flakes easily when tested with fork. (Allow 5 minutes for each ½ inch of thickness.) If more than 1 inch thick, turn when half done. Drain pineapple, reserving ¼ cup juice. Place fruit around fish last 3 minutes of broiling. Heat together ¼ cup butter and reserved juice. Stir in parsley; pass with fish. Makes 4 servings.

Herbed Fish Fillets

1	pound fresh *or* frozen fish fillets
3	tablespoons butter *or* margarine, softened
1	tablespoon chopped green onion
½	teaspoon dried sage, crushed
¼	teaspoon dried thyme, crushed
⅛	teaspoon paprika
1	tablespoon snipped parsley

Thaw fish, if frozen. Separate into fillets or cut into 4 serving-size portions. Place in greased shallow baking pan. Combine softened butter or margarine, green onion, sage, thyme, paprika, ¼ teaspoon *salt,* and ⅛ teaspoon *pepper.* Spread over fish. Broil 4 inches from heat till fish flakes easily when tested with fork. (Allow 5 minutes for each ½ inch of thickness.) Baste occasionally with butter mixture during broiling. If more than 1 inch thick, turn when fish is half done. Sprinkle with parsley. Makes 4 servings.

Foil-Barbecued Shrimp

2	pounds fresh *or* frozen large shrimp, shelled and deveined
6	tablespoons butter
½	cup snipped parsley
¾	teaspoon curry powder
1	clove garlic, minced
½	teaspoon salt
	Dash pepper

Thaw shrimp, if frozen. In saucepan melt butter; stir in parsley, curry powder, garlic, salt, and pepper. Add shrimp; stir to coat. Divide shrimp mixture equally among six 18x12-inch pieces of heavy-duty foil. Fold foil around shrimp, sealing the edges well.

Grill shrimp over *hot* coals about 8 minutes. Turn and grill 7 to 8 minutes more or till done. Serve in foil packages, if desired. Makes 6 servings.

5 OFF THE SHELF

Even when eaten straight out of the can or just slightly cooked, fish and seafood dishes can rouse your sense of taste. Main dishes, salads, and appetizers are all in this collection of recipes that require only minimal cooking.

Guacamole Salad Bowl

1 ripe medium avocado
  Lemon juice
¼ cup milk
1 tablespoon lemon juice
½ cup dairy sour cream
⅓ cup salad oil
½ teaspoon sugar
½ teaspoon chili powder
¼ teaspoon bottled hot pepper
    sauce
  Dash garlic powder
6 cups torn lettuce
1 12½-ounce can tuna, chilled,
    drained, and flaked
1 cup cherry tomatoes, halved
1 cup corn chips
½ cup bias-sliced celery
½ cup shredded cheddar cheese
⅓ cup chopped green onion

Cut avocado in half; remove seed and peel. Mash enough avocado pulp to make ½ cup. Chop any remaining avocado and dip in a little lemon juice to prevent darkening.

To make salad dressing in mixing bowl, food processor, or blender container combine mashed avocado, milk, 1 tablespoon lemon juice, sour cream, salad oil, sugar, chili powder, hot pepper sauce, garlic powder and ¼ teaspoon *salt*. Beat with electric mixer or process in food processor or blender till mixture is smooth. Stir in chopped avocado.

In large salad bowl just before serving toss together torn lettuce, tuna, cherry tomatoes, corn chips, celery, cheddar cheese, and green onion. Serve with salad dressing. Makes 4 main dish servings.

Apple-Tuna Toss

½ cup mayonnaise *or* salad
    dressing
2 tablespoons sliced green onion
2 teaspoons soy sauce
1 teaspoon lemon juice
1 6½-ounce can tuna
4 cups torn salad greens
2 cups chopped apple
1 11-ounce can mandarin orange
    sections, drained
½ cup cashews

Combine mayonnaise or salad dressing, green onion, soy sauce, and lemon juice. Refrigerate several hours. Chill tuna; drain and break into large chunks.

In large salad bowl combine torn salad greens, apple, orange sections, cashews, and tuna; toss together. Pour mayonnaise mixture over salad; toss gently to mix. Makes 4 to 6 side dish servings.

Cucumber-Tuna Boats

2 medium cucumbers
1 6½-ounce can tuna, chilled,
    drained, and flaked
¾ cup shredded American
    cheese (3 ounces)
½ cup finely chopped celery
⅓ cup mayonnaise
2 tablespoons sweet pickle relish
1 tablespoon finely chopped
    onion
1 teaspoon lemon juice
  Paprika

Cut cucumbers in half lengthwise; scrape out seeds. Cut a thin slice from bottom of each cucumber half so cucumber will stand steady; sprinkle cavities with a little salt. Combine tuna, cheese, celery, mayonnaise, pickle relish, onion, and lemon juice. Fill cucumber shells with tuna mixture. Sprinkle with paprika. Makes 4 main dish servings.

Enjoy a "south-of-the-border" flavor by making *Guacamole Salad Bowl.*

Polynesian Shrimp Bowl

1	15¼-ounce can pineapple chunks (juice pack)
2	teaspoons cornstarch
1½	teaspoons curry powder
¼	teaspoon salt
2	teaspoons lemon juice
⅓	cup mayonnaise *or* salad dressing
⅓	cup dairy sour cream
2	cups medium noodles, cooked, drained, and chilled
2	4½-ounce cans shrimp, rinsed and drained
½	cup sliced water chestnuts
¼	cup chopped green pepper

Drain pineapple, reserving juice. Set pineapple aside. In small saucepan combine cornstarch, curry powder, and salt. Stir in reserved pineapple juice. Cook and stir over medium heat till thickened and bubbly; stir in lemon juice. Cool. Stir in mayonnaise or salad dressing and sour cream.

In salad bowl combine pineapple chunks, noodles, shrimp, water chestnuts, and green pepper. Pour curry mixture over; toss gently. Chill thoroughly. Makes 4 main dish servings.

Shrimp-Avocado Salad

1	small avocado
½	cup buttermilk *or* sour milk
1	3-ounce package cream cheese
1	tablespoon lemon juice
1	small clove garlic
½	teaspoon salt
¼	teaspoon bottled hot pepper sauce
6	cups torn lettuce
1	pound fresh *or* frozen shelled shrimp, cooked and drained
18	cherry tomatoes, halved
4	ounces Swiss cheese
	Pepper

Cut avocado in half; remove the seed. Peel avocado and cut into pieces. In blender container place avocado, buttermilk or sour milk, cream cheese, lemon juice, garlic clove, salt, and hot pepper sauce. Cover and blend till smooth. In salad bowl arrange lettuce, shrimp, and tomatoes. Cut cheese into strips; arrange atop. Sprinkle with a little pepper. Toss with avocado mixture to serve. Makes 6 main dish servings.

Spinach-Shrimp Salad

⅓	cup salad oil
1	tablespoon sugar
2	teaspoons vinegar
¼	teaspoon finely shredded orange peel
3	tablespoons orange juice
⅛	teaspoon salt
⅛	teaspoon dry mustard
2	drops bottled hot pepper sauce
10	ounces spinach, torn (6 cups)
1	pound fresh *or* frozen shrimp in shells, cooked, shelled, deveined, halved lengthwise, and chilled
3	oranges, peeled and sectioned
2	kiwi, peeled and sliced
¼	cup slivered almonds, toasted (optional)

For dressing, in screw-top jar combine salad oil, sugar, vinegar, orange peel, orange juice, salt, mustard, and hot pepper sauce. Shake well and chill.

In large salad bowl arrange torn spinach, chilled shrimp, orange sections, and kiwi slices. Sprinkle with almonds, if desired. To serve, shake dressing well; pour over salad and toss to coat. Makes 4 main dish servings.

Marinated Scallop Salad

¾ **pound fresh** *or* **frozen scallops**
1 **cup water**
1 **tablespoon lemon juice**
½ **teaspoon salt**
1 **bay leaf**
1 **9-ounce package frozen French-style green beans**
4 **tiny new potatoes** *or* **2 small potatoes**
2 **tablespoons Italian salad dressing**
½ **cup sliced celery**
1 **tablespoon sliced green onion**
¼ **cup mayonnaise** *or* **salad dressing**
2 **tablespoons dairy sour cream**
1 **tablespoon Italian salad dressing**
½ **teaspoon prepared horseradish**
¼ **teaspoon dried dillweed**
Lettuce
2 **tomatoes, cut into wedges**

Thaw scallops, if frozen. Cut any large scallops in half. In saucepan bring water, lemon juice, salt, and bay leaf to boiling; add scallops and return to boiling. Simmer 1 minute. Drain scallops; discard bay leaf.

Cook green beans according to package directions; drain and cool. Cook potatoes in boiling salted water till tender; drain and cool slightly. While still warm, peel potatoes and cut into ¼-inch-thick slices. Combine warm potatoes with scallops and green beans; toss with 2 tablespoons Italian dressing to coat. Chill at least 2 hours. Add celery and onion to scallop mixture.

Stir together mayonnaise or salad dressing, sour cream, 1 tablespoon Italian salad dressing, horseradish, and dillweed. Toss mayonnaise mixture with scallop mixture. Serve on individual lettuce-lined plates; top with tomato wedges. Garnish with hard-cooked egg or lemon wedges, if desired. Makes 4 main dish servings.

Scallop Chef's Salad

¾ **pound fresh** *or* **frozen scallops**
1 **clove garlic, halved**
4 **cups torn lettuce**
3 **cups torn romaine**
1 **cup sliced celery**
4 **ounces mozzarella cheese, cut into thin strips**
12 **cherry tomatoes, halved**
Thousand island salad dressing

Thaw scallops, if frozen. Cook scallops in boiling salted water for 1 minute or till scallops are opaque; drain and chill.

Rub salad bowl with cut side of garlic; discard garlic. In bowl combine lettuce, romaine, celery, cheese, and tomatoes. Top with chilled scallops. Pour dressing over; toss to combine. Makes 6 main dish servings.

Crab-Stuffed Avocados

1 **pound crab legs, cooked, chilled, and shelled,** *or* **one 7-ounce can crab meat, chilled and drained**
2 **hard-cooked eggs, chopped**
¼ **cup chopped celery**
¼ **cup mayonnaise** *or* **salad dressing**
1 **teaspoon dry mustard**
¼ **teaspoon salt**
Dash Worcestershire sauce
4 **medium avocados**
Lemon juice

Break crab meat into pieces, removing any cartilage. Set aside several larger pieces for garnish. Combine remaining crab meat, eggs, celery, mayonnaise or salad dressing, mustard, salt, and Worcestershire sauce; chill.

Halve avocados lengthwise and remove seeds. Brush cut surfaces with a little lemon juice to prevent darkening. Cut a thin slice from the bottom of each half so avocado will stand steady. Fill avocado halves with crab mixture. Top with reserved crab meat. Serve on lettuce-lined plates, if desired. Makes 4 main dish servings.

Dilled Salmon-Macaroni Salad

½ cup elbow macaroni
¼ cup chopped cucumber
2 tablespoons chopped green pepper
2 tablespoons sliced green onion
⅓ cup mayonnaise *or* salad dressing
½ teaspoon dried dillweed
¼ teaspoon salt
⅛ teaspoon pepper
1 7¾-ounce can salmon, drained, slightly flaked, and skin and bones removed
Lettuce
1 hard-cooked egg, cut into wedges

Cook macaroni in boiling salted water about 8 minutes or till just tender; drain well. In mixing bowl combine cooked macaroni, cucumber, green pepper, and green onion. Stir in mayonnaise or salad dressing, dillweed, salt, and pepper; mix well. Fold in salmon. Season to taste with additional salt and pepper. Cover and chill at least 2 hours.

Spoon salmon mixture into 2 individual lettuce-lined salad bowls. Arrange egg wedges atop each salad. Makes 2 main dish servings.

Salmon-Fruit Mold

2 envelopes unflavored gelatin
2 tablespoons sugar
1½ cups cold water
¼ cup lemon juice
1 cup mayonnaise *or* salad dressing
1 cup dairy sour cream
1 7¾-ounce can salmon, drained, flaked, and skin and bones removed
1 8-ounce can crushed pineapple
1 medium banana, thinly sliced (1 cup)
¾ cup chopped celery

In saucepan combine gelatin and sugar; stir in water. Stir over low heat till gelatin and sugar are dissolved; cool. Stir in lemon juice. In large bowl combine mayonnaise or salad dressing and sour cream; gradually stir in cooled gelatin mixture till smooth. Chill till partially set.

Fold in flaked salmon, *undrained* pineapple, banana slices, and celery. Pour into a 6- or 6½-cup mold; chill till firm. Makes 8 side dish servings.

Crab-Fruit Mold: Prepare recipe as above, *except* substitute one 7-ounce can *crab meat,* drained, flaked and cartilage removed, for the canned salmon.

Lobster-Fruit Mold: Prepare recipe as above, *except* substitute one 5-ounce can *lobster,* drained and flaked, for the canned salmon.

Salmon-Stuffed Tomatoes

1 9-ounce package frozen artichoke hearts
1 15½-ounce can salmon, drained
3 hard-cooked eggs, chopped
1 cup sliced fresh mushrooms
¼ teaspoon salt
Dash pepper
6 large tomatoes
1 cup dairy sour cream
¼ cup diced cucumber
¼ cup milk
1 tablespoon lemon juice
2 teaspoons snipped fresh dillweed *or* ½ teaspoon dried dillweed
¼ teaspoon salt

Cook frozen artichoke hearts according to package directions; drain and chop. Remove skin and bones from salmon; break salmon into chunks. In mixing bowl combine chopped artichoke hearts, salmon, eggs, mushrooms, ¼ teaspoon salt, and pepper; cover and chill.

To prepare tomato cups, cut a thin slice from the stem end of each tomato. Remove core, if present. Use a spoon to scoop out the seeds, leaving a ½-inch-thick shell. If desired, cut top edge into scallops or a sawtooth pattern. Sprinkle tomatoes with a little salt; invert and chill.

For dressing, combine sour cream, cucumber, milk, lemon juice, dillweed, and ¼ teaspoon salt; cover and chill. Toss dressing with salmon mixture.

To serve, place tomato cups right-side-up on serving plate; fill with salmon mixture. Makes 6 main dish servings.

Rice and Tuna Salad

⅔ cup long grain rice *or* quick-
    cooking barley
1 6½-ounce can tuna
1 cup shredded carrot
1 cup sliced celery
2 tablespoons finely chopped
    green onion
½ cup mayonnaise *or* salad
    dressing
2 teaspoons lemon juice
¼ teaspoon poppy seed
¼ teaspoon Worcestershire
    sauce

Cook rice or barley according to package directions; drain. Drain tuna and break into chunks; add to rice or barley along with shredded carrot, sliced celery, and green onion. Cover and chill at least 4 hours. Stir together mayonnaise or salad dressing, lemon juice, poppy seed, Worcestershire sauce, and ¼ teaspoon *salt*. Just before serving, toss mayonnaise mixture with salad. Garnish with carrot curls and parsley, if desired. Makes 4 side dish servings.

Tuna Salad in Tomato Cups

1 6½-ounce can tuna
½ cup sliced celery
¼ cup sliced green onion
¼ cup sliced pimiento-stuffed
    olives
1 tablespoon lemon juice
¼ teaspoon salt
    Dash pepper
2 hard-cooked eggs, chopped
½ cup mayonnaise *or* salad
    dressing
4 medium tomatoes
    Lettuce

Drain tuna and flake meat. In mixing bowl combine tuna, celery, green onion, olives, lemon juice, salt, and pepper. Gently stir in chopped egg and mayonnaise or salad dressing; cover and chill.

To prepare tomato cups, cut a thin slice from the stem end of each tomato. Remove core, if present. Use a spoon to scoop out the seeds, leaving a ½-inch-thick shell. If desired, cut top edge into scallops or a sawtooth pattern. Sprinkle tomatoes with a little salt; invert and chill.

To serve, place tomatoes on individual lettuce-lined plates; sprinkle with salt. Fill each tomato with about *½ cup* tuna mixture. Garnish with parsley, olives, or hard-cooked egg slices, if desired. Makes 4 side dish servings.

Salad Niçoise

½ cup salad oil
3 tablespoons lemon juice
2 tablespoons vinegar
½ teaspoon salt
½ teaspoon dry mustard
½ teaspoon paprika
½ teaspoon dried basil, crushed
4 cups torn romaine
1 head bibb lettuce, torn
1 12½-ounce can tuna (water
    pack), chilled and drained
1 9-ounce package frozen
    French-style green beans,
    cooked, drained, and chilled
2 medium tomatoes, cut into
    wedges
3 hard-cooked eggs, cut into
    wedges
¼ cup sliced pitted ripe olives
1 2-ounce can anchovy fillets,
    drained

For dressing, in screw-top jar combine salad oil, lemon juice, vinegar, salt, dry mustard, paprika, and basil. Close jar and shake well to mix. Chill.

In large salad bowl place romaine and lettuce. Break tuna into chunks; mound in center of lettuce. Arrange green beans, tomato wedges, and egg wedges around tuna. Garnish with olives and anchovies. Shake dressing again to mix; pass with salad. Makes 6 main dish servings.

Try the traditional *Crab Louis,* named by Enrico Caruso in honor of a Seattle chef,
at your next luncheon. Or, create the more unusual *Tossed Tuna Salad* to serve your guests.

Tossed Tuna Salad

10 ounces spinach, torn (6 cups)
1 9¼-ounce can tuna, chilled, drained, and broken into large pieces
2 oranges, peeled and sectioned
1 cup fresh bean sprouts
½ cup sliced water chestnuts
2 tablespoons sliced green onion
½ cup Italian salad dressing

In large salad bowl combine spinach, tuna, orange sections, bean sprouts, water chestnuts, and green onion. Pour Italian dressing over mixture and toss. Makes 4 main dish servings.

Crab Louis

¼ cup whipping cream
1 cup mayonnaise *or* salad dressing
¼ cup chili sauce
¼ cup chopped green pepper
2 tablespoons sliced green onion
1 teaspoon lemon juice
¼ teaspoon salt
4 lettuce cups
1 large head lettuce, shredded
2 to 3 cups chilled, cooked crab meat *or* two 7-ounce cans crab meat, chilled and drained, *or* one 7-ounce can crab meat plus 1½ cups flaked, cooked fish fillets, drained and chilled
2 large tomatoes, cut into wedges
2 hard-cooked eggs, sliced
Pitted ripe olives (optional)
Kiwi slices (optional)

Whip cream to soft peaks. Fold in mayonnaise or salad dressing, chili sauce, chopped green pepper, sliced green onion, lemon juice, and salt. Chill mixture thoroughly.

Line 4 salad plates with lettuce cups. Place shredded lettuce atop cups. If necessary, remove cartilage from crab meat. Arrange chunks of crab meat or crab meat and flaked fish atop the shredded lettuce.

Arrange tomato wedges and egg slices around crab meat. Sprinkle with a little salt. Pour ¼ *cup* mayonnaise mixture over *each* salad. If desired garnish with ripe olives and kiwi slices; pass remaining dressing. Makes 4 main dish servings.

Shrimp-Tomato Vinaigrette

1 pound peeled and deveined shrimp, cooked
1 6-ounce package frozen pea pods, thawed
2 tablespoons sliced green onion
¼ cup salad oil
2 tablespoons dry white wine
2 tablespoons white vinegar
1 .6-ounce envelope Italian salad dressing mix
1 to 2 teaspoons drained capers
Dash pepper
4 medium tomatoes
Lettuce

In mixing bowl combine shrimp, pea pods, and green onion. In screw-top jar combine salad oil, wine, vinegar, dry Italian salad dressing mix, capers, and pepper; cover and shake well to mix. Pour dressing over shrimp mixture. Cover and refrigerate several hours.

To make tomato cups, place each tomato stem side down on a cutting board. With sharp knife, cut tomatoes into 4 to 6 wedges, cutting to the base of the tomato but not through it. Spread wedges slightly to form petals; sprinkle lightly with salt. Cover and chill.

To serve, place tomato cups on lettuce-lined salad plates. Drain shrimp-vegetable mixture; spoon into tomato cups. Makes 4 main dish servings.

Open-Faced Tuna Sandwiches

1   9¼-ounce can tuna
¾   cup sliced celery
¾   cup mayonnaise *or* salad
    dressing
½   cup shredded cheddar cheese
⅓   cup slivered almonds, toasted
¼   cup sliced pitted ripe olives
2   teaspoons lemon juice
4   English muffins, split

Drain and flake tuna. Combine flaked tuna, celery, mayonnaise or salad dressing, cheese, almonds, olives, and lemon juice; toss lightly. Spread each English muffin half with about ⅓ *cup* tuna mixture.

Preheat baking sheet in 350° oven for 5 minutes. Place English muffins on preheated pan. Bake in 350° oven for 10 minutes. Makes 4 servings.

Salmon Salad Sandwiches

1   7¾-ounce can salmon
½   cup dairy sour cream
¼   cup thinly sliced celery
¼   cup chopped pecans
½   teaspoon lemon juice
¼   teaspoon dried dillweed
¼   teaspoon salt
8   slices whole wheat bread
    Butter *or* margarine
    Lettuce leaves
    Fresh bean sprouts (optional)

Drain salmon; flake meat, removing skin and bones. In mixing bowl combine salmon, sour cream, celery, pecans, lemon juice, dillweed, and salt. Chill.

Spread whole wheat bread slices lightly with butter or margarine on one side. Top four bread slices with salmon mixture, lettuce leaves, bean sprouts, and remaining bread slices. Cut sandwiches in half diagonally. Makes 4 servings.

Lox and Bagels

3   bagels
1   3-ounce package cream
    cheese, softened
8   ounces sliced smoked red
    salmon (lox)

Split bagels horizontally. Toast bagels, if desired. Spread cut surfaces generously with softened cream cheese. Arrange salmon slices (lox) on the 6 halves. Serve with lemon wedges or freshly ground pepper, if desired. Serve whole, or cut into small wedges and serve for appetizers. Makes 6 open-faced sandwiches.

Swedish Pickled Shrimp

1   pound fresh *or* frozen medium
    shrimp in shells
½   cup celery tops
¼   cup mixed pickling spice
1   tablespoon salt
1   small onion, sliced
2   bay leaves
1   cup salad oil
1   cup white vinegar
3   tablespoons capers
2½ teaspoons celery seed
1½ teaspoons salt
    Few drops bottled hot pepper
    sauce

Cover shrimp with boiling water; add celery tops, pickling spice, and 1 tablespoon salt. Cover and simmer 5 minutes. Drain; peel and devein shrimp referring to illustrations on page 39.

In plastic bag set in a deep bowl combine shrimp, onion, and bay leaves. Combine salad oil, vinegar, *undrained* capers, celery seed, 1½ teaspoons salt, and hot pepper sauce. Pour oil mixture over shrimp. Close bag; chill at least 24 hours, turning bag occasionally. Makes 6 appetizer servings.

Shrimp Cocktail

1 **pound fresh** *or* **frozen shelled shrimp, cooked and chilled**
Lettuce
¼ **cup Cocktail Sauce**
Lemon wedges

Arrange chilled shrimp in 4 lettuce-lined sherbet dishes. Spoon some Cocktail Sauce atop each serving. Garnish each with lemon wedges. Makes 4 servings.

Cocktail Sauce: Combine ¾ cup *chili sauce*, 2 tablespoons *lemon juice*, 1 tablespoon prepared *horseradish*, 2 teaspoons *Worcestershire sauce*, ½ teaspoon grated *onion*, and a few dashes *bottled hot pepper sauce*; mix well. Chill thoroughly.

Sardine Appetizer Spread

1 **3¾-ounce can sardines in oil, drained**
¼ **cup butter** *or* **margarine, softened**
2 **tablespoons finely chopped green onion**
2 **tablespoons chili sauce**
1 **tablespoon lemon juice**
¼ **teaspoon dry mustard**
Few drops bottled hot pepper sauce
Crisp rye crackers

Mash sardines with a fork. Combine sardines with butter or margarine, onion, chili sauce, lemon juice, dry mustard, and hot pepper sauce; mix well. Chill. Let stand at room temperature for 20 to 30 minutes before serving. Serve with crisp rye crackers. Makes about 1 cup spread.

Anchovy Dip

1 **8-ounce package cream cheese, softened**
¼ **cup milk**
2 **tablespoons chopped pimiento-stuffed olives**
1 **tablespoon anchovy paste**
1 **tablespoon sliced green onion**
1 **teaspoon lemon juice**
¼ **teaspoon Worcestershire sauce**
Assorted raw vegetables

In small mixer bowl combine softened cream cheese, milk, chopped olives, anchovy paste, sliced green onion, lemon juice, and Worcestershire sauce. Beat at medium speed of electric mixer till light and fluffy; chill. Serve with raw vegetable dippers. Makes 1½ cups dip.

Crab Dip

1 **8-ounce package cream cheese, softened**
¼ **cup mayonnaise**
3 **to 4 tablespoons milk**
⅛ **teaspoon garlic powder**
⅛ **teaspoon bottled hot pepper sauce**
1 **6-ounce can crab meat, drained, flaked, and cartilage removed**
Snipped chives
Assorted raw vegetables *or* **chips**

In small mixer bowl beat together cream cheese, mayonnaise, milk, garlic powder, hot pepper sauce, and dash *salt*. Stir in crab meat; chill. Garnish with snipped chives. Serve with vegetable dippers or chips. Makes 2 cups.

Party Tuna Spread

2 3-ounce packages cream
   cheese with chives, softened
2 teaspoons lemon juice
1 teaspoon Worcestershire
   sauce
⅛ teaspoon onion powder
   Dash bottled hot pepper sauce
1 6½-ounce can tuna, drained
   and finely flaked *or* one 7¾-
   ounce can salmon, drained,
   finely flaked, and skin and
   bones removed
¼ cup finely chopped celery
   Party rye bread
   Sliced pimiento-stuffed olives

In mixing bowl combine softened cream cheese with chives, lemon juice, Worcestershire sauce, onion powder, and hot pepper sauce. Stir in finely flaked tuna or salmon and celery; mix well. Chill several hours or overnight. To serve, spread about *1 tablespoon* mixture on a slice of party rye; garnish with olive slices. Makes 1½ cups.

Salmon and Sour Cream Spread

1 15½-ounce can salmon, chilled
¼ cup mayonnaise *or* salad
   dressing
2 tablespoons lemon juice
¼ teaspoon garlic salt
¼ teaspoon dried dillweed
¼ teaspoon Worcestershire
   sauce
⅛ teaspoon cayenne
1 cup dairy sour cream
½ cup finely chopped zucchini *or*
   cucumber
2 tablespoons thinly sliced
   green onion
2 tablespoons drained capers
   Melba toast rounds

Drain salmon; break up with a fork, removing bones and skin. In bowl combine mayonnaise or salad dressing, lemon juice, garlic salt, dillweed, Worcestershire sauce, and cayenne. Stir in salmon.

   In separate bowl combine sour cream, zucchini or cucumber, green onion, and capers. To serve, spread salmon mixture over melba toast rounds; top with sour cream mixture. Makes about 7 dozen appetizers.

Egg and Caviar Spread

4 hard-cooked eggs, finely
   chopped
⅔ cup sour cream with French
   onion
2 tablespoons butter *or*
   margarine, softened
¾ teaspoon prepared mustard
¼ teaspoon salt
   Dash pepper
1 tablespoon finely chopped
   celery
1 2-ounce jar caviar
1 tablespoon snipped parsley
   Assorted crackers

In small mixer bowl beat together the chopped eggs, ¼ *cup* of the sour cream, butter or margarine, mustard, salt, and pepper till well blended. Stir in the celery. Spread egg mixture on a flat serving platter, making a layer about 1 inch thick. Chill till firm. To serve, spread remaining sour cream over egg layer. Top with caviar and snipped parsley. Serve with crackers. Makes about 1½ cups.

Shrimp-Cheese Balls

2 3-ounce packages cream
cheese, softened
1½ teaspoons prepared mustard
1 teaspoon finely chopped onion
1 teaspoon lemon juice
Dash cayenne
Dash salt
1 4½-ounce can shrimp
⅔ cup chopped cashews or
walnuts
Assorted crackers

In bowl combine cream cheese, mustard, onion, lemon juice, cayenne, and salt; mix well. Drain shrimp; break into pieces. Stir shrimp into cheese mixture; chill.

Form shrimp mixture into ½-inch balls; roll in chopped cashews or walnuts. (Or, form shrimp mixture into 1 large ball; press nuts over outside of ball to coat.) Chill. Serve with assorted crackers. Makes 40 appetizers.

Oyster Pâté

1 pint shucked oysters
¼ cup mayonnaise or salad
dressing
2 tablespoons butter or
margarine
1 tablespoon lemon juice
2 teaspoons finely chopped
onion
½ teaspoon salt
½ teaspoon dry mustard
Few drops bottled hot pepper
sauce
1 teaspoon unflavored gelatin
2 tablespoons cold water
1 hard-cooked egg, finely
chopped
Finely snipped parsley
Assorted crackers

In covered saucepan cook oysters in their liquid over medium heat for about 2 minutes or till edges curl; drain. In blender container combine oysters, mayonnaise or salad dressing, butter or margarine, lemon juice, chopped onion, salt, mustard, and hot pepper sauce. Cover and blend till smooth.

In small bowl soften gelatin in cold water. Place bowl in larger pan of hot water; stir till gelatin dissolves. Stir into oyster mixture. Turn into a small mold. Chill several hours. Unmold carefully. Garnish with chopped hard-cooked egg and parsley. Serve with crackers. Makes about 1¼ cups.

Creamy Shrimp Salad Pie

Plain Pastry for Single-Crust
Pie (see recipe, page 30)
1 3-ounce package cream
cheese, softened
1 envelope unflavored gelatin
½ cup cold water
1 cup boiling water
⅓ cup mayonnaise or salad
dressing
2 tablespoons lemon juice
½ cup whipping cream
1 4½-ounce can shrimp, rinsed,
drained, and cut up
½ cup chopped celery
¼ cup chopped green pepper
2 tablespoons chopped pimiento
1 teaspoon finely chopped onion

Roll out pastry and line a 9-inch pie plate. Trim pastry ½ inch beyond edge of pie plate, flute edge; do not prick bottom. Bake in 450° oven for 10 to 12 minutes. Cool. Beat cream cheese till fluffy. Soften gelatin in cold water. Add boiling water to gelatin, stirring to dissolve. Gradually add gelatin mixture to cream cheese, beating well. Add mayonnaise or salad dressing and lemon juice; beat smooth. Chill till consistency of corn syrup, stirring occasionally.

Whip cream to soft peaks; set aside. When gelatin is consistency of unbeaten egg whites (partially set), beat 2 to 3 minutes or till slightly fluffy. Fold in whipped cream, shrimp, celery, green pepper, pimiento, and onion. If necessary, chill mixture again till mixture mounds. Pour into baked pastry shell. Chill till firm. Garnish with additional shrimp and parsley, if desired. Makes 12 appetizer servings.

Serve elegant hors d'oeuvres such as *Shrimp-Dill Mousse*, *Clam-Stuffed Cheese Ball*, *Cheese-Crab Dip*, or *Shrimp Tartlets*. Seafood's delicate flavor is appreciated in this form.

Shrimp-Dill Mousse

½ cup chilled tomato juice
2 envelopes unflavored gelatin
1 cup boiling tomato juice
2 cups dairy sour cream
2 tablespoons lemon juice
1½ teaspoons dried dillweed
½ teaspoon Worcestershire sauce
1 4½-ounce can shrimp, drained
Lettuce
Assorted crackers *or* party rye
bread slices

Add ½ cup chilled tomato juice and gelatin to blender container; cover and blend on low speed till gelatin is softened. Add boiling tomato juice; blend on low speed till gelatin dissolves. If granules cling to sides, stop blender and use rubber spatula to push into liquid.

Turn blender to high speed; add sour cream, lemon juice, dillweed, Worcestershire sauce and ½ teaspoon *salt*. Blend till smooth. Stop blender and add shrimp. Turn blender on and off several times just till shrimp are chopped. Pour into 5-cup mold. Chill 4 hours or till firm. Unmold onto lettuce-lined plate; serve with crackers. Makes about 4 cups.

Cheese-Shrimp Dip

1 8-ounce package cream
cheese, softened
3 to 4 tablespoons milk
2 tablespoons dry sherry
¼ teaspoon prepared horseradish
1 4½-ounce can shrimp, drained
and finely chopped
2 tablespoons sliced green onion
2 tablespoons chopped pimiento
Assorted raw vegetables

In mixing bowl beat together softened cream cheese, milk, sherry, and horseradish. Fold in shrimp, green onion, and pimiento. Turn mixture into serving bowl; cover and chill. Serve with vegetable dippers. Makes 1¾ cups.

Cheese-Crab Dip: Prepare recipe as above *except* substitute one 6-ounce can *crab meat,* drained, flaked and cartilage removed, for the shrimp.

Clam-Stuffed Cheese Ball

1 whole Gouda *or* Edam cheese
(about 1 pound)
1 cup dairy sour cream
3 7½-ounce cans minced clams
¼ cup milk
2 tablespoons snipped parsley
1 tablespoon finely chopped hot
pepper (1 small)
¼ teaspoon onion powder
Assorted crackers

Bring cheese to room temperature. Cut off top of cheese and remove. Carefully scoop out cheese, leaving ¼-inch shell. Shred cheese top and scooped-out cheese; beat together shredded cheese and sour cream with electric mixer till smooth.

Drain clams, reserving ¼ cup liquid. Stir clams, reserved liquid, milk, parsley, pepper, and onion powder into whipped cheese mixture. Mound into cheese shell, reserving any extra to refill shell as used. Chill. Top with more snipped parsley, if desired. Serve with assorted crackers. Makes 4 cups.

Shrimp Tartlets

Plain Pastry for Double-Crust
Pie (see recipe, page 30)
1 3-ounce package cream
cheese, softened
¼ cup dairy sour cream
2 tablespoons cocktail sauce
1½ teaspoons snipped fresh
dillweed *or* ½ teaspoon
dried dillweed
2 4½-ounce cans shrimp
⅓ cup finely chopped celery

Form pastry dough into a ball. Roll to about ⅛-inch thickness; cut into 2-inch squares. Place squares in 1¾-inch diameter muffin pans, pressing to fit. Prick with fork. Bake in 400° oven for 8 to 10 minutes or till golden. Cool.

Meanwhile, beat together softened cream cheese, sour cream, cocktail sauce, and dill. Rinse and drain shrimp. Coarsely chop shrimp; stir shrimp and celery into cream cheese mixture. Chill thoroughly. To serve, spoon a rounded teaspoonful shrimp mixture into each tart shell. Garnish with fresh dill, if desired. Makes 4 to 5 dozen appetizers.

Crab Appetizer Puffs

1 **pound fresh crab meat,**
    cooked, *or* 1 pound frozen
    crab meat
½ **cup butter *or* margarine**
1 **cup boiling water**
1 **cup all-purpose flour**
¼ **teaspoon salt**
4 **eggs**
¼ **cup mayonnaise *or* salad**
    dressing
¼ **cup dairy sour cream**
¼ **cup chili sauce**
1 **teaspoon prepared**
    horseradish
    Few drops bottled hot pepper
    sauce
¼ **cup sliced celery**
2 **tablespoons thinly sliced**
    green onion

Thaw crab meat, if frozen. Remove any cartilage from crab meat and flake meat; set aside. In saucepan melt butter or margarine in the boiling water. Add flour and salt all at once, stirring vigorously. Cook and stir till mixture forms a ball that does not separate. Remove pan from heat; cool 10 minutes. Add eggs, one at a time, beating after each addition till batter is smooth.

Drop by rounded teaspoonfuls 2 inches apart on greased baking sheet. Bake in 400° oven for 10 to 15 minutes or till golden brown and puffy. Remove from oven; split puffs. Cool on a wire rack.

In bowl combine mayonnaise or salad dressing, sour cream, chili sauce, prepared horseradish, and bottled hot pepper sauce. Stir in crab meat, celery, and green onion. Fill each puff with about *1 tablespoon* of the crab mixture. Makes 30 appetizers.

Oysters Rockefeller

24 **oysters in shells**
    Rock salt *or* crumpled
    aluminum foil
1 **10-ounce package frozen**
    chopped spinach, cooked
    and drained
2 **tablespoons chopped onion**
2 **tablespoons snipped parsley**
2 **tablespoons butter *or***
    margarine, melted
½ **teaspoon salt**
    Several drops bottled hot
    pepper sauce
    Dash pepper
¼ **cup fine dry bread crumbs**
    (1 slice)
1 **tablespoon butter *or***
    margarine, melted

Open oyster shells. With a knife, remove oysters from shells and pat oysters dry with paper toweling. Wash the shells. Place one oyster in the deep half of each oyster shell.

Line a shallow baking pan with rock salt to about ½-inch depth or use aluminum foil to keep shells from tipping. Arrange oysters in shells on the salt or foil.

Press all excess water from cooked spinach. In mixing bowl combine drained spinach, chopped onion, snipped parsley, 2 tablespoons butter or margarine, salt, bottled hot pepper sauce, and pepper. Spread about *1 tablespoon* of spinach mixture over each oyster in shell.

In small bowl toss together the fine dry bread crumbs and 1 tablespoon melted butter or margarine. Sprinkle each oyster with about ½ teaspoon of the buttered crumbs. Bake oysters in 425° oven for about 10 minutes or till done. Makes 24 appetizers.

Angels on Horseback

8 **slices bacon**
16 **shucked oysters (about ½ pint)**
16 **saltine crackers**
    Lemon wedges

Cut each bacon slice in half crosswise. Partially cook the bacon; drain on paper toweling. Drain oysters. Wrap one half slice of partially cooked bacon around each oyster; secure each with a wooden pick.

Place oysters on rack in shallow baking pan. Bake in 450° oven for 10 to 15 minutes or till bacon is crisp and oysters are done. Place one bacon-wrapped oyster on each cracker. Serve with hot lemon wedges. Makes 16 appetizers.

INDEX

T-W

Tips